Playing In Art

Edited by Lacey Belinda Smith

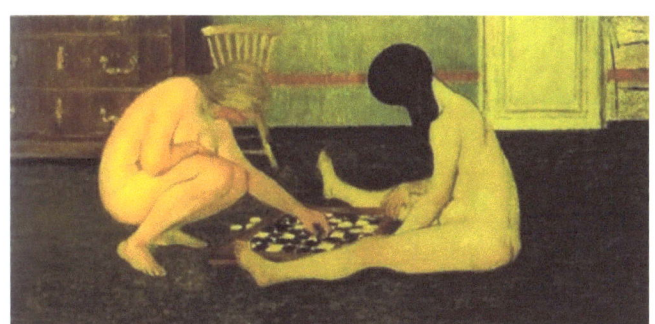

Alice Bailly (1872 – 1938) was a radical Swiss painter that was known for her interpretation of cubism and her multimedia wool paintings.

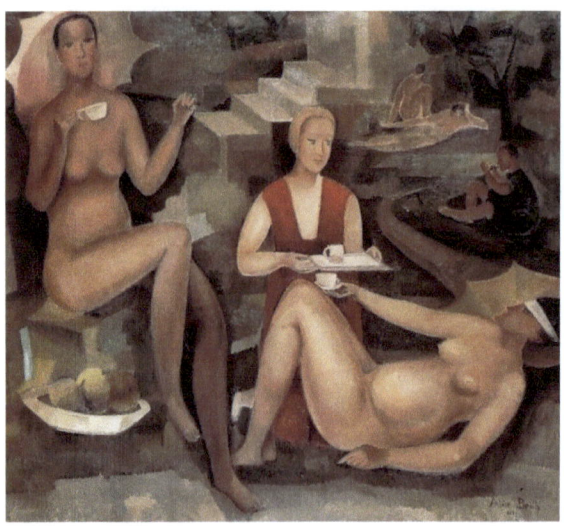

Afternoon Tea--Alice Bailly--1927

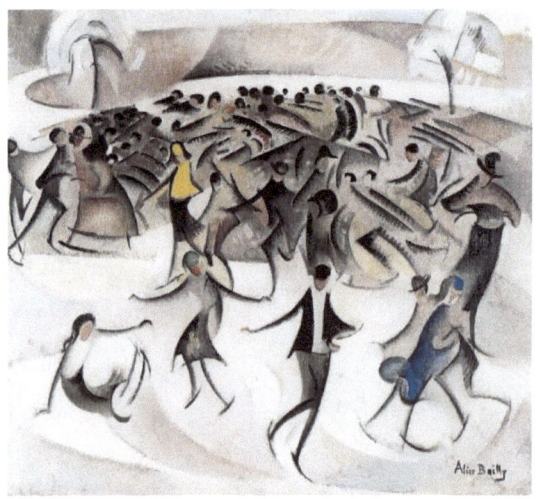

Skating in the Bois de Boulogne--Alice Bailly--1913

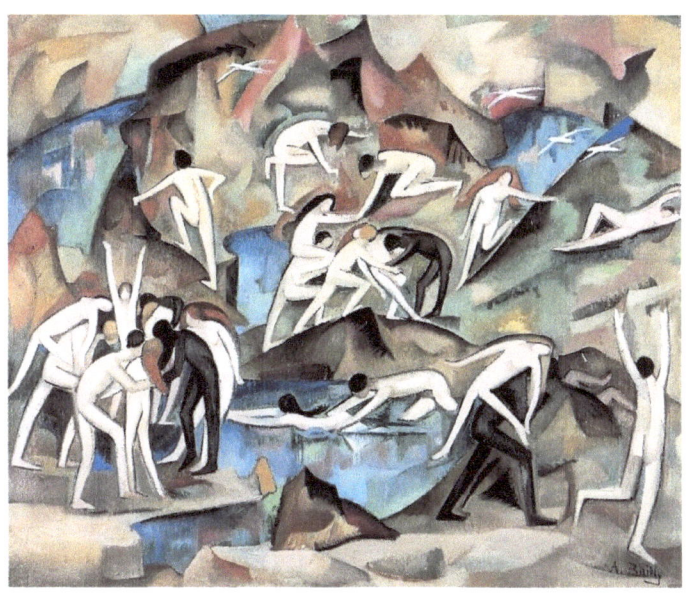

Bacchanale among the Rocks--Alice Bailly--1912

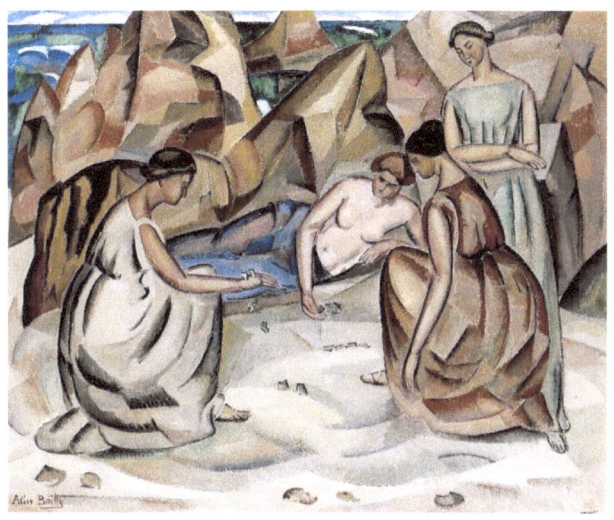

Les Joueuses d'osselets--Alice Bailly--1912

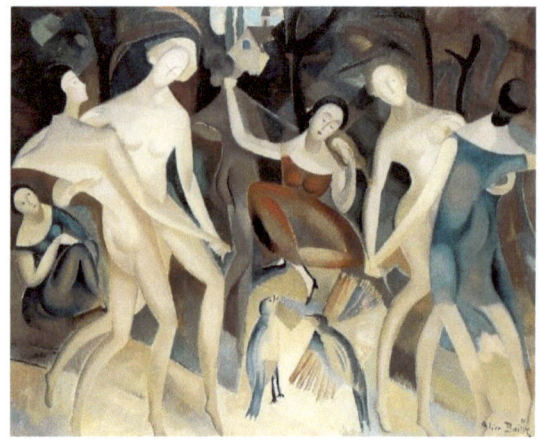

Joy in the Forest--Alice Bailly – 1922

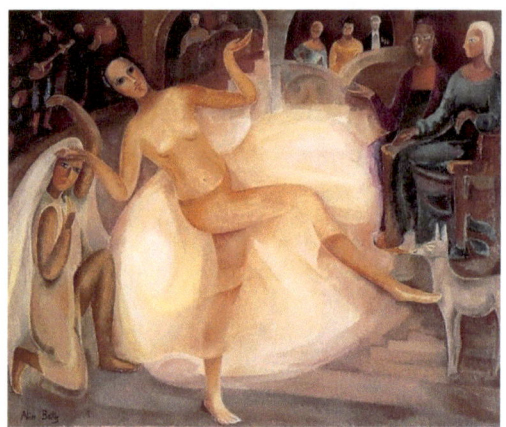

Dancer at the Palais--Alice Bailly--1928

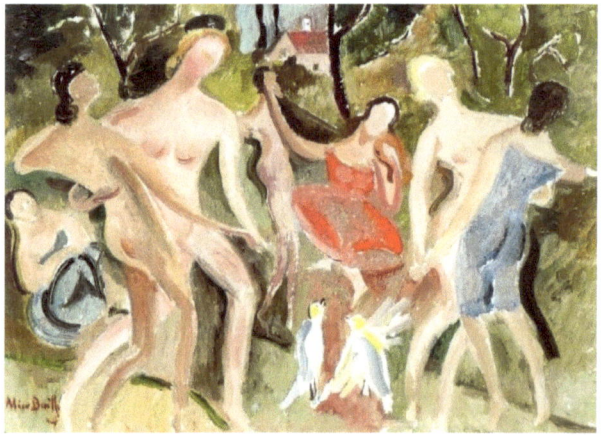

Dancers (Beautiful Caprice)--Alice Bailly--1918

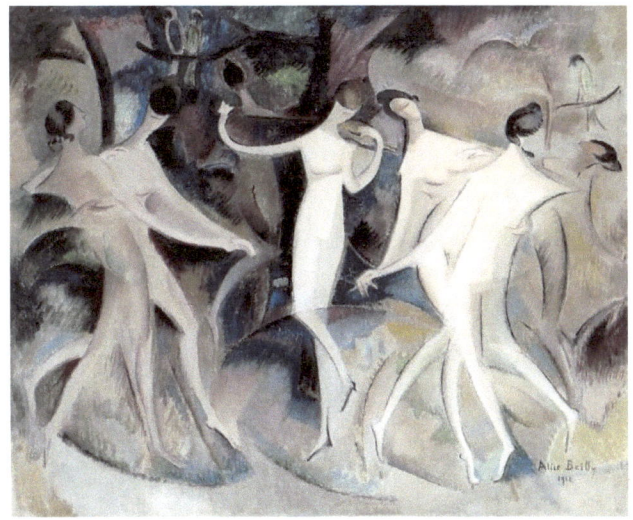

Le caprice des Belles--Alice Bailly--1918

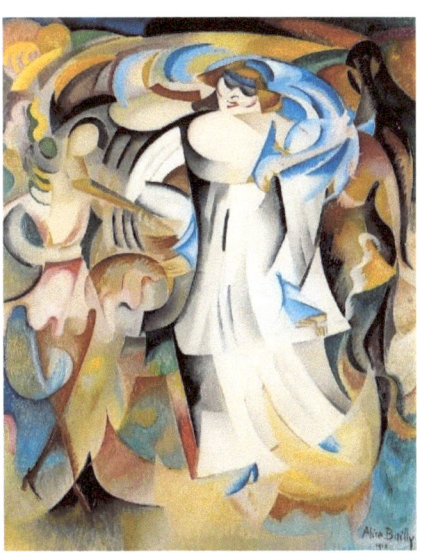

Marval at the Van Dongen's Masked Ball--Alice Bailly--1914

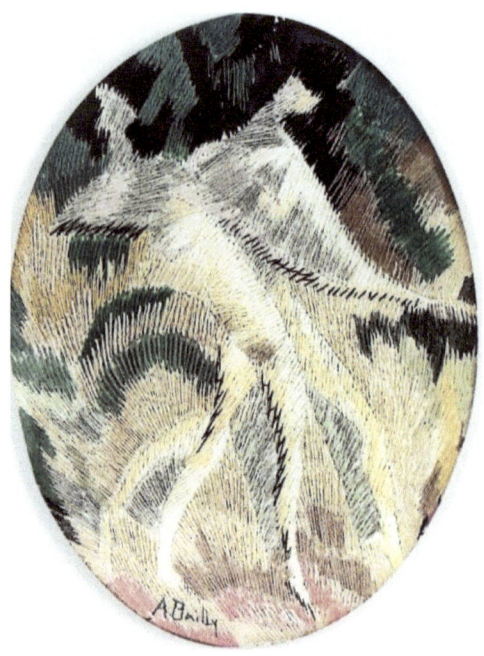

Momentum (Dance Rhythms)--Alice Bailly--1918

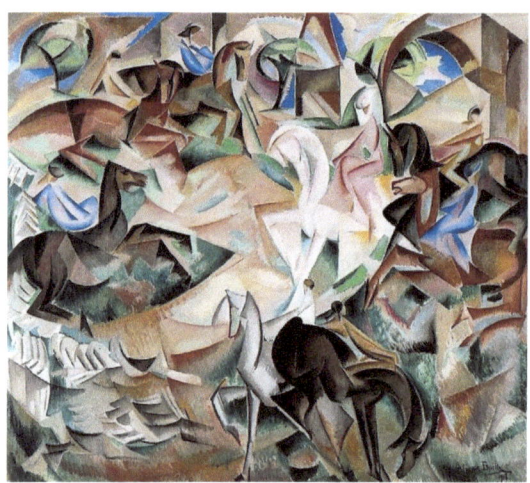

Equestrian Fantasy With Pink Lady--Alice Bailly--1913

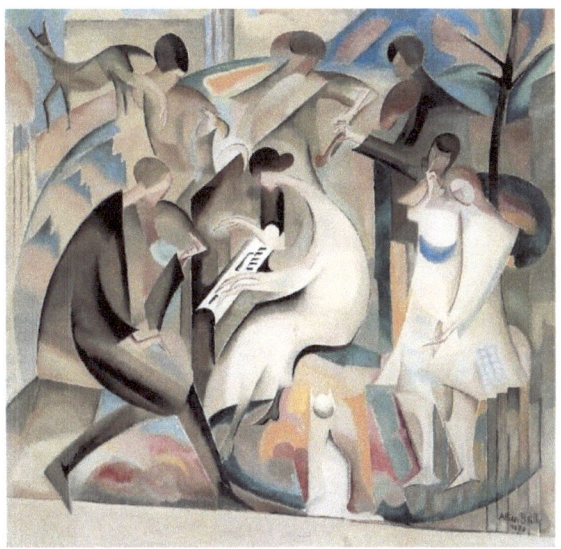

A Concert in the Garden--Alice Bailly--1920

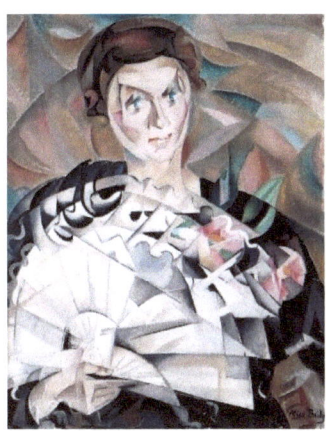

Playing with a Fan (Portrait of Louisa Bally, the Artist's Sister)—Alice Bailly

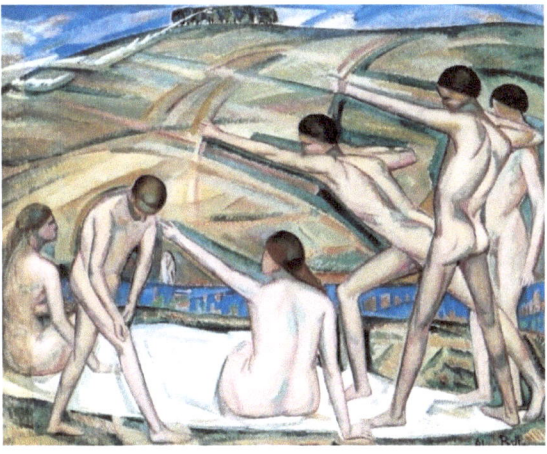

Archers--Alice Bailly--1911

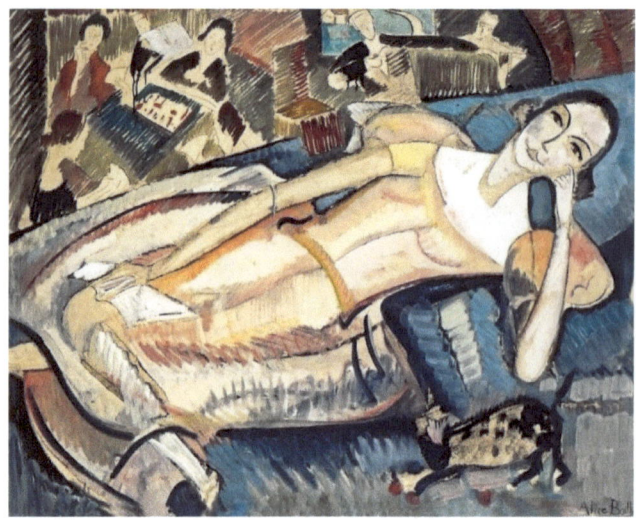

At Leisure (Portrait of Wilma Toosby)--Alice Bailly--1922

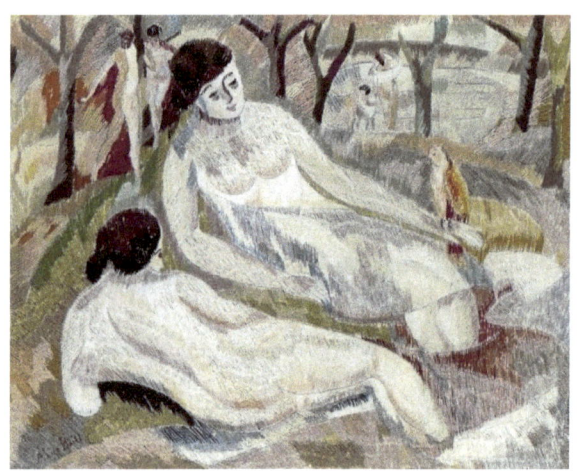

Autumn Afternoon--Alice Bailly

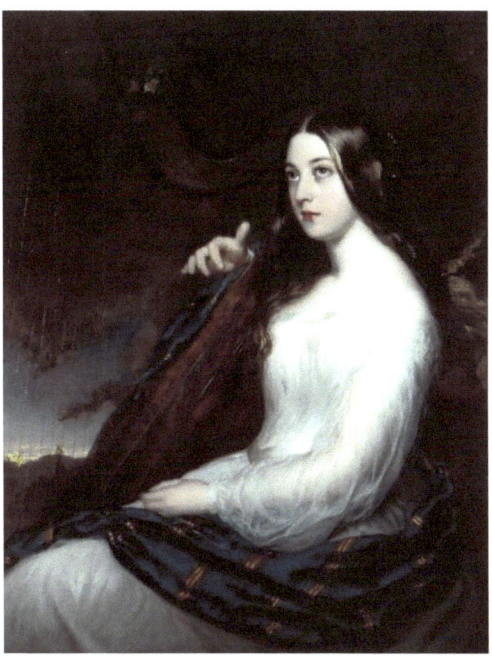

Playing the Harp--William Beechey

My Gentle Harp

My gentle Harp, once more I waken
The sweetness of thy slumbering strain;
In tears our last farewell was taken,
And now in tears we meet again.
No light of joy hath o'er thee broken,
But, like those harps whose heavenly skill
Of slavery, dark as thine, hath spoken,
Thou hang'st upon the willows still.

And yet, since last thy chord resounded,
An hour of peace and triumph came,
And many an ardent bosom bounded
With hopes -- that now are turn'd to shame.
Yet even then, while Peace was singing
Her halcyon song o'er land and sea,
Though joy and hope to others bringing,
She only brought new tears to thee.

Then, who can ask for notes of pleasure,
My drooping Harp, from chords like thine?
Alas, the lark's gay morning measure
As ill would suit the swan's decline!
Or how shall I, who love, who bless thee,
Invoke thy breath for Freedom's strains,
When even the wreaths in which I dress thee
Are sadly mix'd -- half flowers, half chains?

But come -- if yet thy frame can borrow
One breath of joy, oh, breathe for me,
And show the world, in chains and sorrow,
How sweet thy music still can be;
How gaily, even 'mid gloom surrounding,
Thou yet canst wake at pleasure's thrill --
Like Memnon's broken image sounding,
'Mid desolation tunefull still!

By Sir Thomas Moore

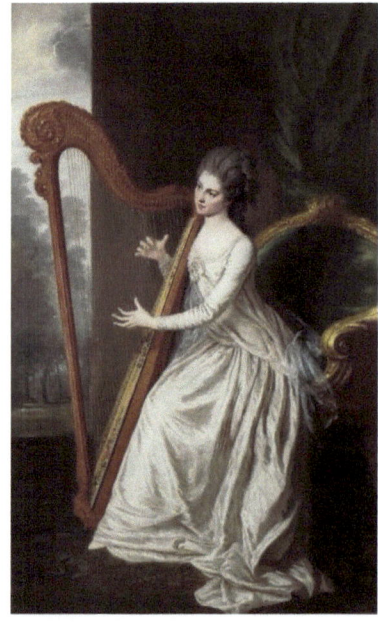

Lady Frances Seymour Conway (1751–1820), Countess of Lincoln--William Hoare

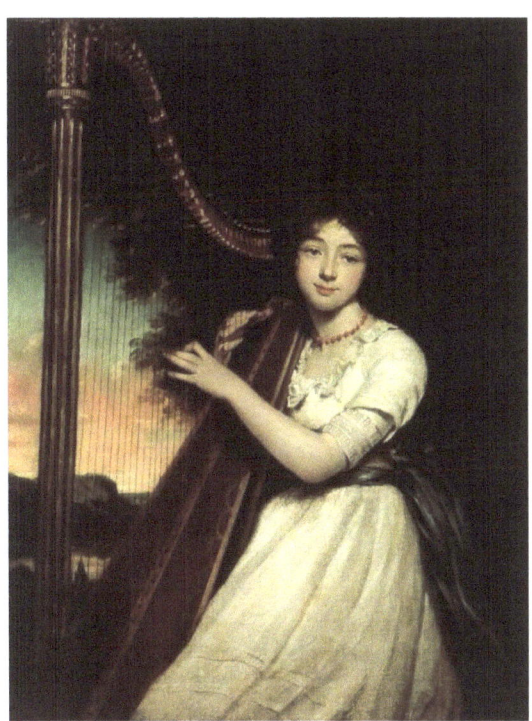

A Young Lady Playing the Harp--James Northcote--1814

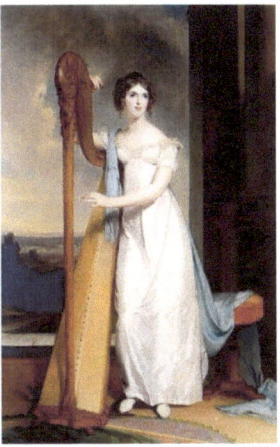

Elizabeth Eichelberger Ridgely (Known As Lady With A Harp)--Thomas Sully—1818--Romanticism

The Lady To Her Guitar

For him who struck thy foreign string,
I ween this heart has ceased to care;
Then why dost thou such feelings bring

To my sad spirit—old Guitar?

It is as if the warm sunlight
In some deep glen should lingering stay,
When clouds of storm, or shades of night,
Have wrapt the parent orb away.

It is as if the glassy brook
Should image still its willows fair,
Though years ago the woodman's stroke
Laid low in dust their Dryad-hair.

Even so, Guitar, thy magic tone
Hath moved the tear and waked the sigh;
Hath bid the ancient torrent moan,
Although its very source is dry.

Emily Jane Brontë

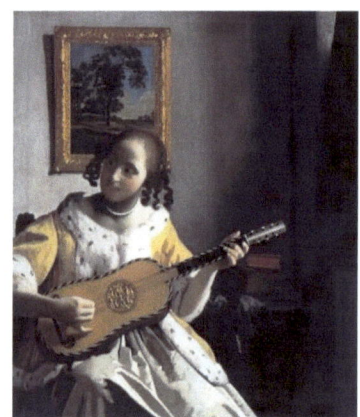

Youg Woman Playing A Guitar--Johannes Vermeer--Baroque

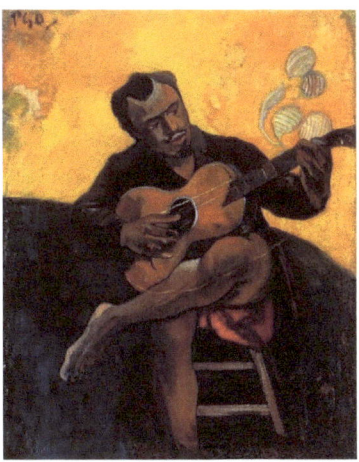

The Guitar Player--Paul Gauguin—1894--Cloisonnism

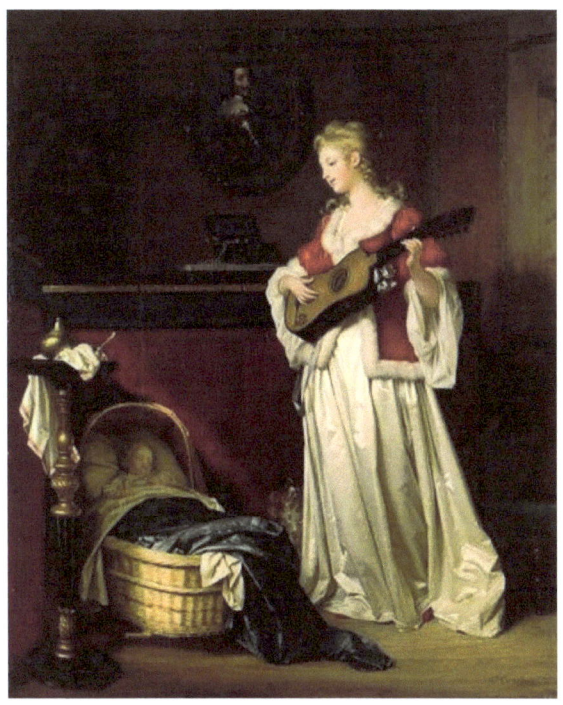

Dors, mon enfant (Sleep my child)--Marguerite Gérard --genre painting

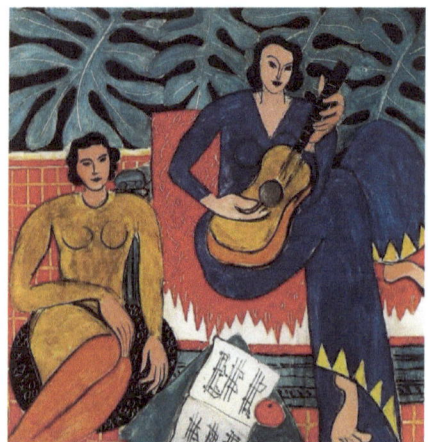

Music-- La Musique)—Henri Matisse—1939--Expressionism

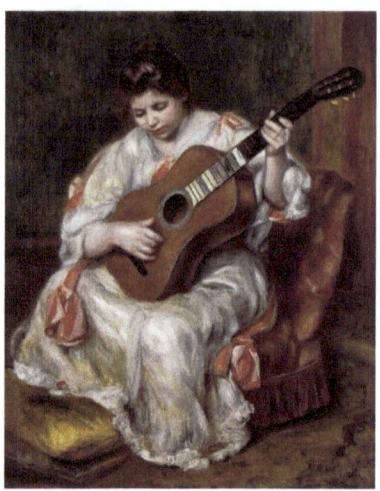

Woman Playing The Guitar--Pierre-Auguste Renoir—1896--Realism

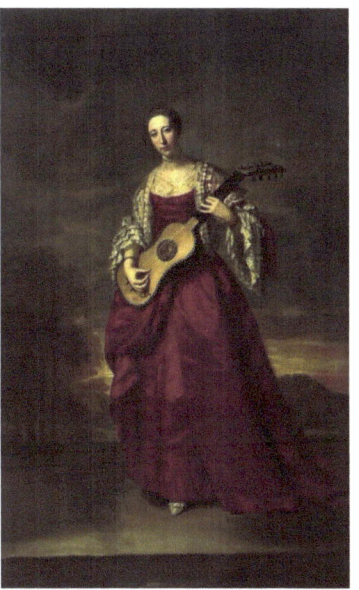

Caroline D'Arcy (d.1778), 4th Marchioness of Lothian-- Adolphe, Joseph Anton

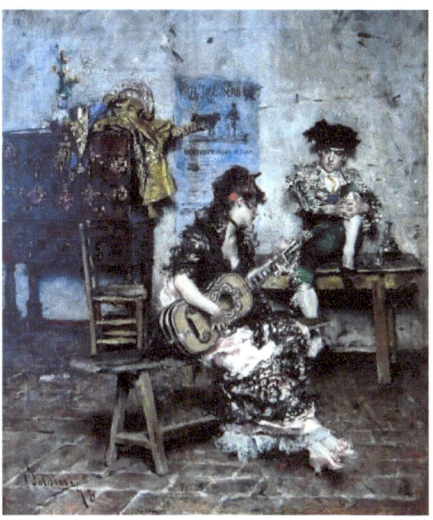

A Guitar Player--Giovanni Boldini—1873--Impressionism

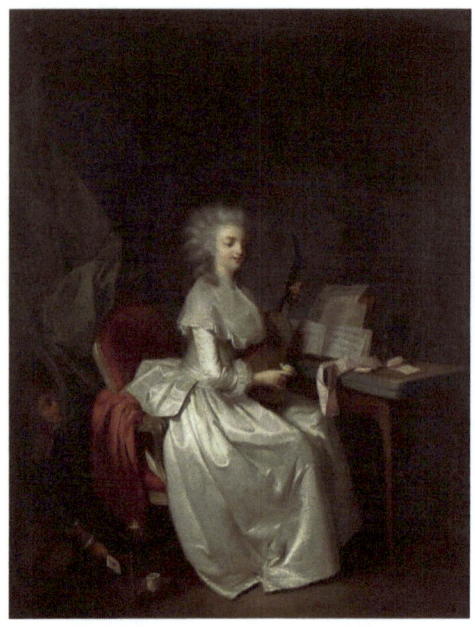

A young Woman playing the Guitar with a Songbird on her Hand--Louis-Léopold Boilly--genre painting

Let Us Play Yesterday

Let Us play Yesterday—
I—the Girl at school—
You—and Eternity—the
Untold Tale—

Easing my famine
At my Lexicon—
Logarithm—had I—for Drink—
'Twas a dry Wine—

Somewhat different—must be—
Dreams tint the Sleep—

Cunning Reds of Morning
Make the Blind—leap—

Still at the Egg-life—
Chafing the Shell—
When you troubled the Ellipse—
And the Bird fell—

Manacles be dim—they say—
To the new Free—
Liberty—Commoner—
Never could—to me—

'Twas my last gratitude
When I slept—at night—
'Twas the first Miracle
Let in—with Light—

Can the Lark resume the Shell—
Easier—for the Sky—
Wouldn't Bonds hurt more
Than Yesterday?

Wouldn't Dungeons sorer frate
On the Man—free—
Just long enough to taste—
Then—doomed new—

God of the Manacle
As of the Free—
Take not my Liberty
Away from Me—

— Emily Dickinson

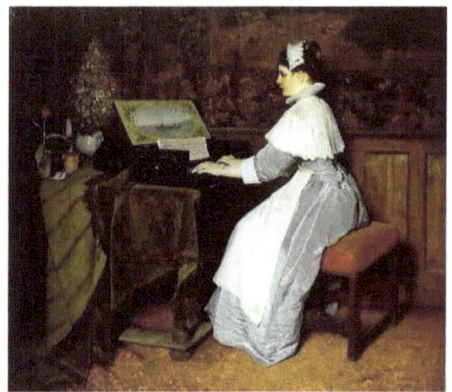

Still Life (Girl At A Spinet)--Gabriel von Max—1871-- Art Nouveau (Modern)

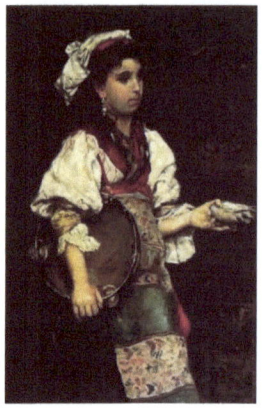

Spanish Girl--Julius LeBlanc Stewart—1875--Realism

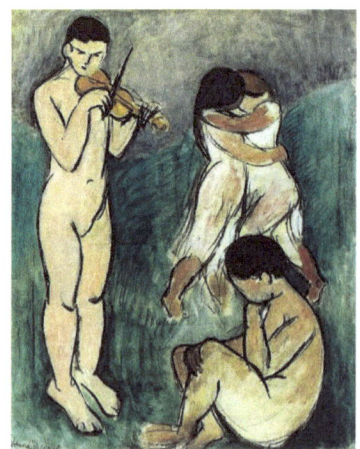

Music (Sketch)--Henri Matisse—1907--Expressionism

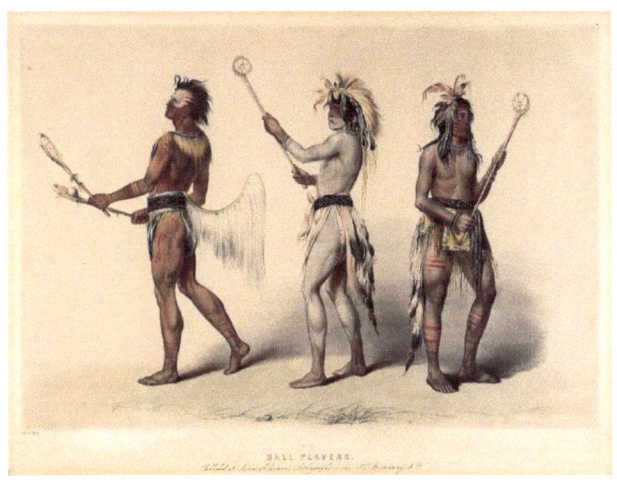

Ball Players--George Catlin-- Realism

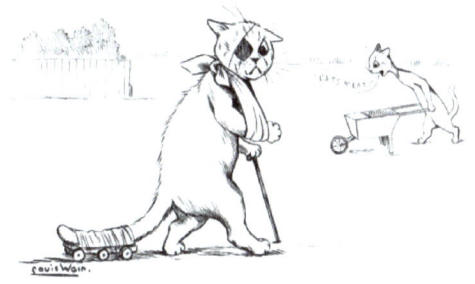

Fter The Football Match You Are Not Lucky, But A Better Time Is Coming--

Louis Wain--Art Nouveau

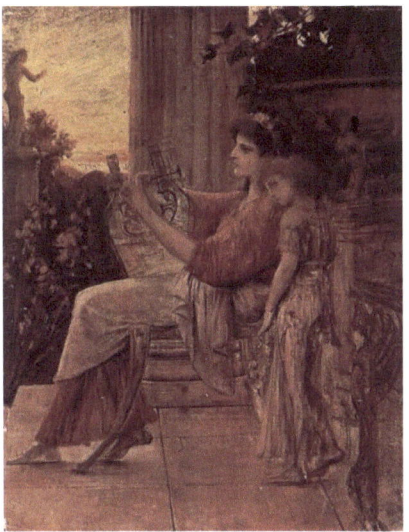

Sappho--Gustav Klimt--Romanticism

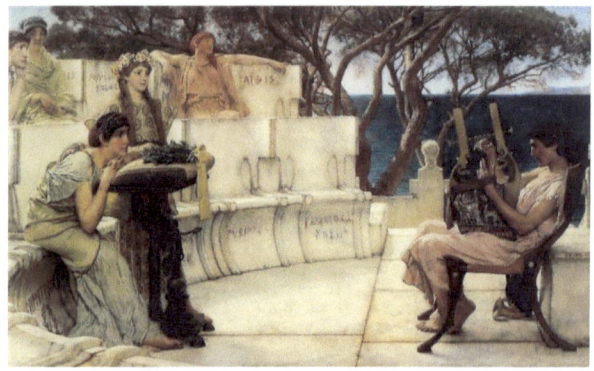

Sappho And Alcaeus--Sir Lawrence Alma-Tadema—1881--Romanticism

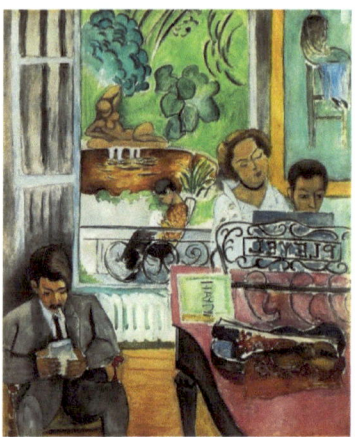

He Music Lesson (La lecon de musique)

--Henri Matisse—1917--Post-Impressionism

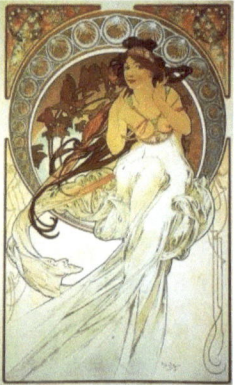

Music--Alphonse Mucha—1898--Art Nouveau

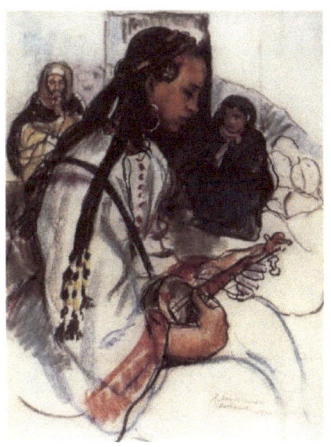

Boy Musician (Мальчик музыкант)--Zinaida Serebriakova—1928--Expressionism

Leisure

What is this life if, full of care,

We have no time to stand and stare.

No time to stand beneath the boughs

And stare as long as sheep or cows.

No time to see, when woods we pass,

Where squirrels hide their nuts in grass.

No time to see, in broad daylight,

Streams full of stars, like skies at night.

No time to turn at Beauty's glance,

And watch her feet, how they can dance.

No time to wait till her mouth can

Enrich that smile her eyes began.

A poor life this if, full of care,

We have no time to stand and stare.

William Henry Davies

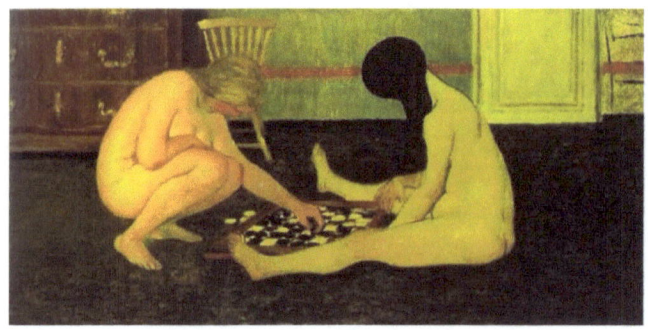

Naked Women Playing Checkers—(Femmes nues jouant aux dames)

Felix Vallotton—1897--Cloisonnism

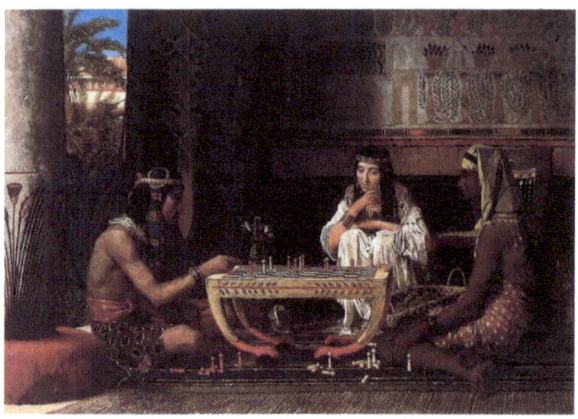

Egyptian Chess Players--Sir Lawrence Alma-Tadema—1865--Romanticism

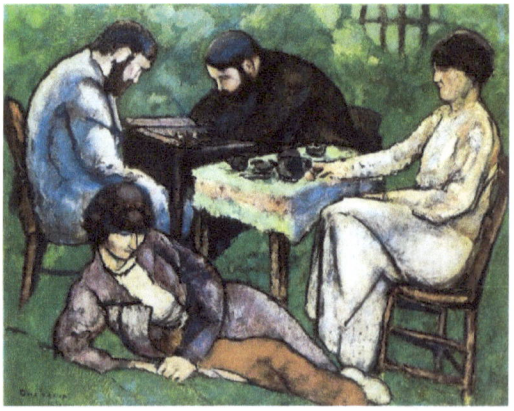

Chess Game--Marcel Duchamp—1910--Post-Impressionism

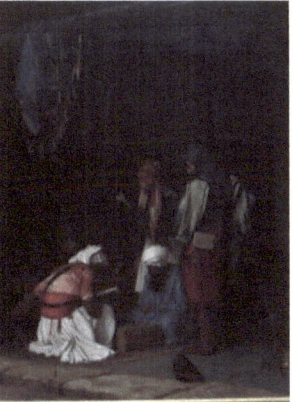

Turkish Bashi Bazouk Mercenaries Playing Chess In A Market Place--Jean-Leon Gerome--Orientalism

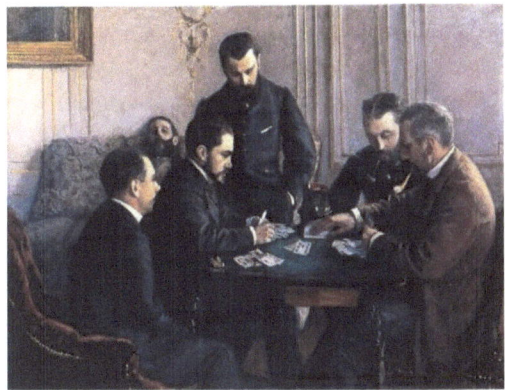

The Bezique Game--Gustave Caillebotte—1880--Impressionism

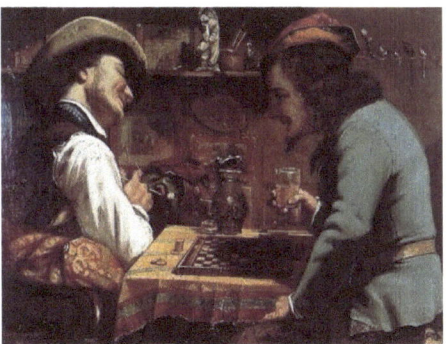

The Draughts Players--Gustave Courbet—1844--Romanticism

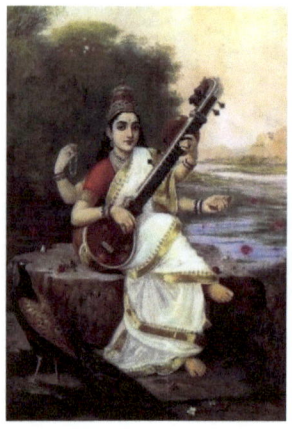

Painting of The goddess Saraswati--Raja Ravi Varma—1896--Academicism

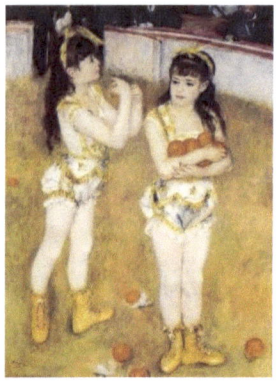

Acrobats At The Cirque Fernando--Pierre-Auguste Renoir—1879--Impressionism

My Lute Awake

My lute awake! perform the last

Labour that thou and I shall waste,

And end that I have now begun;

For when this song is sung and past,

My lute be still, for I have done.

As to be heard where ear is none,

As lead to grave in marble stone,

My song may pierce her heart as soon;

Should we then sigh or sing or moan?
No, no, my lute, for I have done.

The rocks do not so cruelly
Repulse the waves continually,
As she my suit and affection;
So that I am past remedy,
Whereby my lute and I have done.

Proud of the spoil that thou hast got
Of simple hearts thorough Love's shot,
By whom, unkind, thou hast them won,
Think not he hath his bow forgot,
Although my lute and I have done.

Vengeance shall fall on thy disdain
That makest but game on earnest pain.
Think not alone under the sun
Unquit to cause thy lovers plain,
Although my lute and I have done.

Perchance thee lie wethered and old
The winter nights that are so cold,
Plaining in vain unto the moon;
Thy wishes then dare not be told;

Care then who list, for I have done.

And then may chance thee to repent

The time that thou hast lost and spent

To cause thy lovers sigh and swoon;

Then shalt thou know beauty but lent,

And wish and want as I have done.

Now cease, my lute; this is the last

Labour that thou and I shall waste,

And ended is that we begun.

Now is this song both sung and past:

My lute be still, for I have done.

Sir Thomas Wyatt

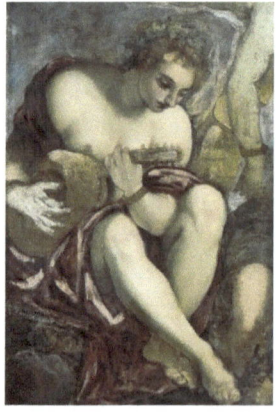

Muse With Lute--Tintoretto—1879--Impressionism

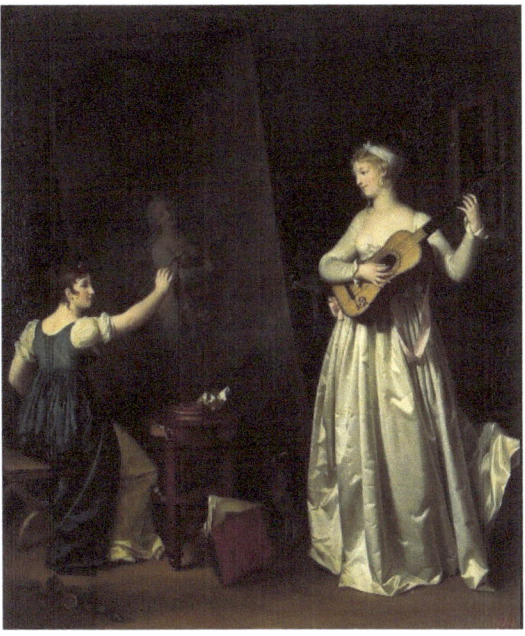

Peintre faisant le portrait d'une joueuse de luth (Painter when painting a portrait of a lute player)--Marguerite Gérard--genre painting

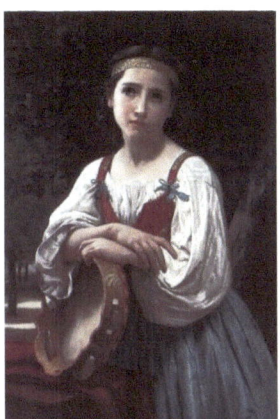

Gypsy Girl With A Basque Drum--William-Adolphe Bouguereau—1867--Neoclassicism

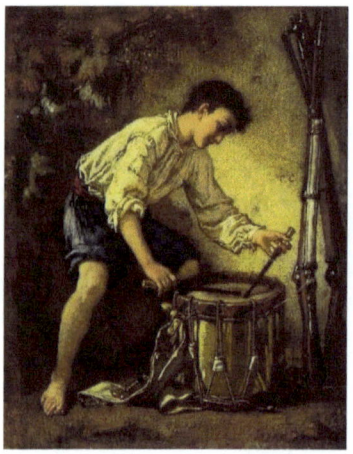

The Young Drummer--Thomas Couture—1857--Romanticism

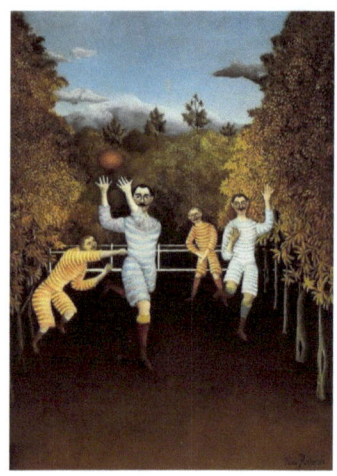

The Football Players--Henri Rousseau—1908--Naïve Art (Primitivism)

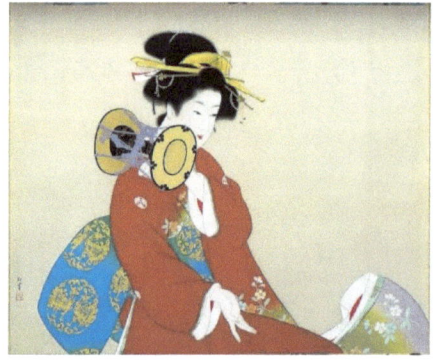

Sound Of Tsuzumi (Tabor or Drum)--Uemura Shoen—1940--Nihonga

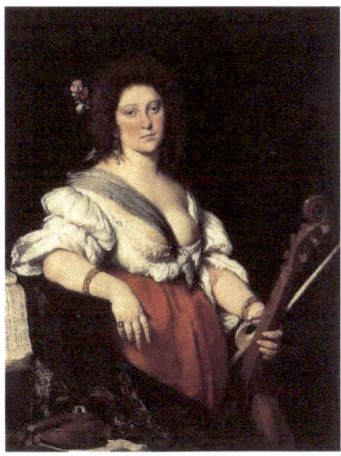

Gamba Player--Bernardo Strozzi--1635--Baroque

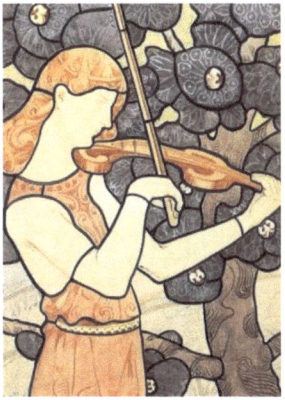

A Música--Eliseu Visconti—1898--Art Nouveau

The Touch of the Master's Hand

'Twas battered and scarred,
And the auctioneer thought it
hardly worth his while
To waste his time on the old violin,
but he held it up with a smile.

"What am I bid, good people", he cried,
"Who starts the bidding for me?"
"One dollar, one dollar, Do I hear two?"
"Two dollars, who makes it three?"
"Three dollars once, three dollars twice, going for three,"

But, No,
From the room far back a gray bearded man
Came forward and picked up the bow,
Then wiping the dust from the old violin
And tightening up the strings,
He played a melody, pure and sweet
As sweet as the angel sings.

The music ceased and the auctioneer
With a voice that was quiet and low,
Said "What now am I bid for this old violin?"
As he held it aloft with its' bow.

"One thousand, one thousand, Do I hear two?"
"Two thousand, Who makes it three?"
"Three thousand once, three thousand twice,
Going and gone", said he.

The audience cheered,
But some of them cried,
"We just don't understand."
"What changed its' worth?"
Swift came the reply.
"The Touch of the Masters Hand."

"And many a man with life out of tune
All battered and bruised with hardship
Is auctioned cheap to a thoughtless crowd
Much like that old violin

A mess of pottage, a glass of wine,
A game and he travels on.
He is going once, he is going twice,
He is going and almost gone.

But the Master comes,
And the foolish crowd never can quite understand,
The worth of a soul and the change that is wrought
By the Touch of the Masters' Hand.

Myra Brooks Welch

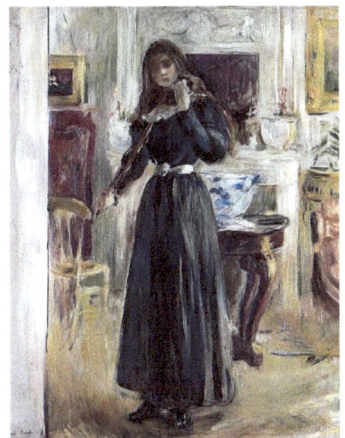

Julie Playing A Violin--Berthe Morisot--Impressionism--genre painting

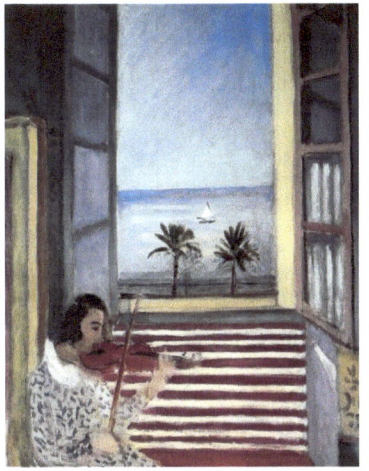

Young Woman Playing Violin--Henri Matisse—1923--Expressionism

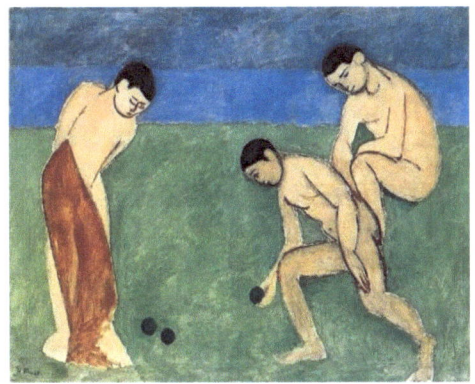

Game of Bowls--Henri Matisse—1908--Expressionism

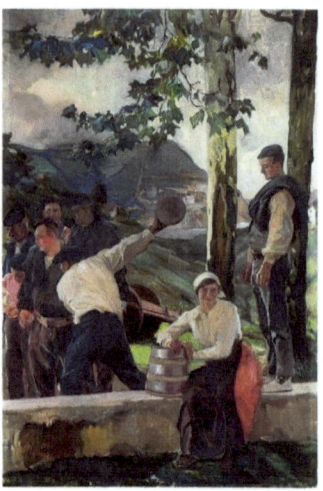

Game Of Skittles--Joaquín Sorolla—1914--Impressionism

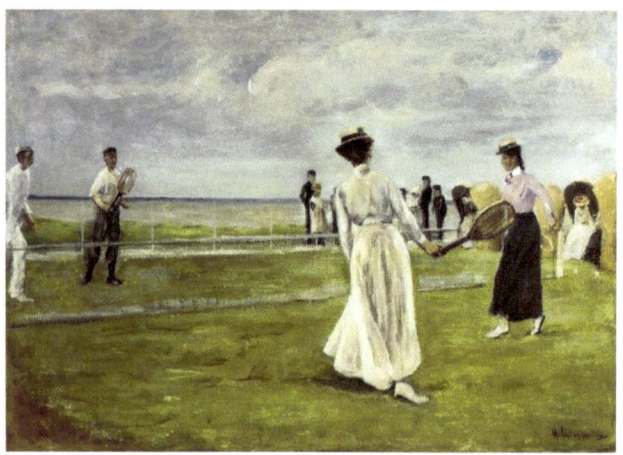

Tennis Game By The Sea--Max Liebermann—1901--Impressionism

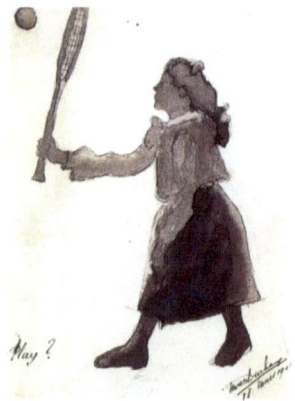

Play--Marcel Duchamp—1902--Expressionism

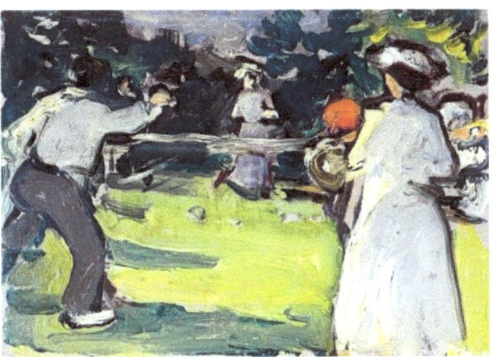

Game Of Tennis, Luxembourg Gardens--Samuel Peploe—1906--Post-Impressionism

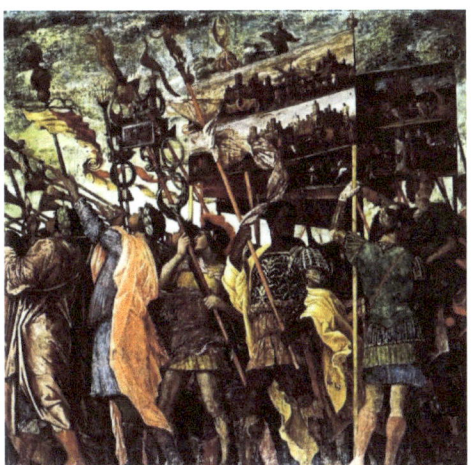

Trumpeters--Andrea Mantegna--High Renaissance

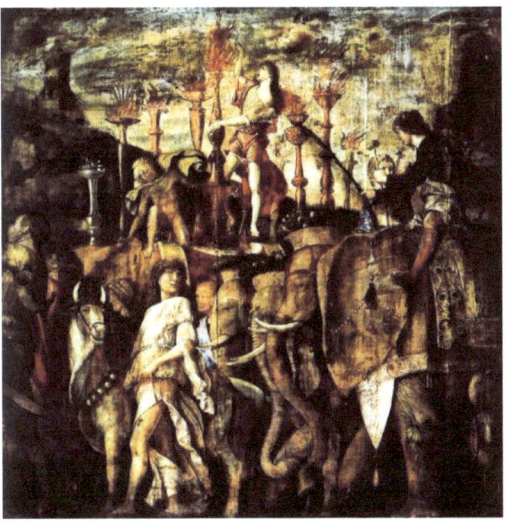

Trumpet Players--Andrea Mantegna--High Renaissance

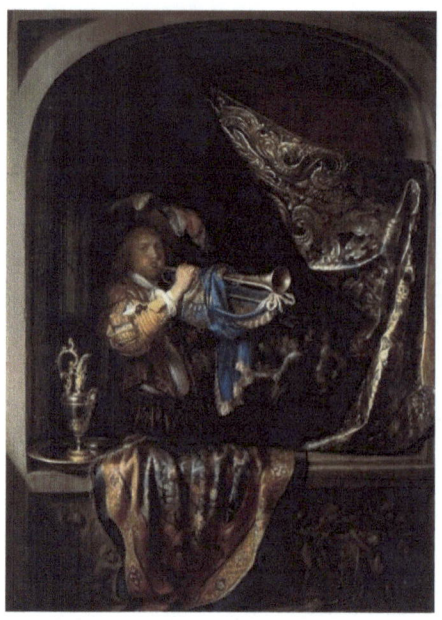

Trumpet Player In Front Of A Banquet--Gerrit Dou--Baroque

A Tale of a Trumpet

"Old woman, old woman, will you go a-shearing?
Speak a little louder, for I'm very hard of hearing."

—Old Ballad.

Of all old women hard of hearing,
The deafest sure was Dame Eleanor Spearing!
On her head, it is true,
Two flaps there grew,
That served for a pair of gold rings to go through,
But for any purpose of ears in a parley,
They heard no more than ears of barley.

No hint was needed from D. E. F.,
You saw in her face that the woman was deaf:
From her twisted mouth to her eyes so peery,
Each queer feature asked a query;
A look that said in a silent way,

"Who? and What? and How? and Eh?
I'd give my ears to know what you say!"

And well she might! for each auricular
Was deaf as a post—and that post in particular
That stands at the corner of Dyott Street now,
And never hears a word of a row!
Ears that might serve her now and then
As extempore racks for an idle pen;
Or to hang with hoops from jewellers' shops;
With coral, ruby, or garnet drops;
Or, provided the owner so inclined,
Ears to stick a blister behind;
But as for hearing wisdom, or wit,
Falsehood, or folly, or tell-tale-tit,
Or politics, whether of Fox or Pitt,
Sermon, lecture, or musical bit,
Harp, piano, fiddle, or kit,
They might as well, for any such wish,
Have been buttered, done brown, and laid in a dish!

She was deaf as a post,—as said before—
And as deaf as twenty similes more,
Including the adder, that deafest of snakes,
Which never hears the coil it makes.

She was deaf as a house—which modern tricks
Of language would call as deaf as bricks—
For her all human kind were dumb,
Her drum, indeed, was so muffled a drum,
That none could get a sound to come,
Unless the Devil, who had Two Sticks!
She was as deaf as a stone—say one of the stones
Demosthenes sucked to improve his tones;
And surely deafness no further could reach
Than to be in his mouth without hearing his speech!

She was deaf as a nut—for nuts, no doubt,
Are deaf to the grub that's hollowing out—

As deaf, alas! as the dead and forgotten—
(Gray has noticed the waste of breath,
In addressing the "dull, cold ear of death"),
Or the felon's ear that is stuffed with cotton—
Or Charles the First in statue quo;
Or the still-born figures of Madame Tussaud,
With their eyes of glass, and their hair of flax,
That only stare whatever you "ax,"
For their ears, you know, are nothing but wax.

She was deaf as the ducks that swam in the pond,
And wouldn't listen to Mrs. Bond,—
As deaf as any Frenchman appears,
When he puts his shoulders into his ears:
And—whatever the citizen tells his son—
As deaf as Gog and Magog at one!
Or, still to be a simile-seeker,
As deaf as dogs'-ears to Enfield's Speaker!

She was deaf as any tradesman's dummy,
Or as Pharaoh's mother's mother's mummy;
Whose organs, for fear of modern sceptics,
Were plugged with gums and antiseptics.

She was deaf as a nail—that you cannot hammer
A meaning into for all your clamour—
There never was such a deaf old Gammer!
So formed to worry
Both Lindley and Murray,
By having no ear for Music or Grammar!

Deaf to sounds, as a ship out of soundings,
Deaf to verbs, and all their compoundings,
Adjective, noun, and adverb, and particle,
Deaf to even the definite article—
No verbal message was worth a pin,
Though you hired an earwig to carry it in!

In short, she was twice as deaf as Deaf Burke,
Or all the Deafness in Yearsley's work,

Who in spite of his skill in hardness of hearing,
Boring, blasting, and pioneering,
To give the dunny organ a clearing,
Could never have cured Dame Eleanor Spearing.

Of course the loss was a great privation,
For one of her sex—whatever her station—
And none the less that the dame had a turn
For making all families one concern,
And learning whatever there was to learn
In the prattling, tattling village of Tringham—
As, who wore silk? and who wore gingham?
And what the Atkins's shop might bring 'em?
How the Smiths contrived to live? and whether
The fourteen Murphys all pigged together?
The wages per week of the Weavers and Skinners,
And what they boiled for their Sunday dinners?
What plates the Bugsbys had on the shelf,
Crockery, china, wooden, or delf?
And if the parlour of Mrs. O'Grady
Had a wicked French print, or Death and the Lady?
Did Snip and his wife continue to jangle?
Had Mrs. Wilkinson sold her mangle?
What liquor was drunk by Jones and Brown?
And the weekly score they ran up at the Crown?
If the cobbler could read, and believed in the Pope?
And how the Grubbs were off for soap?
If the Snobbs had furnished their room upstairs,
And how they managed for tables and chairs,
Beds, and other household affairs,
Iron, wooden, and Staffordshire wares?
And if they could muster a whole pair of bellows?
In fact she had much of the spirit that lies
Perdu in a notable set of Paul Prys,
By courtesy called Statistical Fellows—
A prying, spying, inquisitive clan,
Who have gone upon much of the self-same plan,

Jotting the labouring class's riches;
And after poking in pot and pan,
And routing garments in want of stitches,
Have ascertained that a working man
Wears a pair and a quarter of average breeches!

But this, alas! from her loss of hearing,
Was all a sealed book to Dame Eleanor Spearing;
And often her tears would rise to their founts—
Supposing a little scandal at play
'Twixt Mrs. O'Fie and Mrs. Au Fait—
That she couldn't audit the gossips' accounts.
'Tis true, to her cottage still they came,
And ate her muffins just the same,
And drank the tea of the widowed dame,
And never swallowed a thimble the less
Of something the reader is left to guess,
For all the deafness of Mrs. S.
Who saw them talk, and chuckle, and cough,
But to see and not share in the social flow,
She might as well have lived, you know,
In one of the houses in Owen's Row,
Near the New River Head, with its water cut off!
And yet the almond oil she had tried,
And fifty infallible things beside,
Hot, and cold, and thick, and thin,
Dabbed, and dribbled, and squirted in:
But all remedies failed; and though some it was clear,
Like the brandy and salt
We now exalt,
Had made a noise in the public ear,
She was just as deaf as ever, poor dear!

At last—one very fine day in June—
Suppose her sitting,
Busily knitting,
And humming she didn't quite know what tune;
For nothing she heard but a sort of whizz,

Which, unless the sound of circulation,
Or of thoughts in the process of fabrication,
By a spinning-jennyish operation,
It's hard to say what buzzing it is.
However, except that ghost of a sound,
She sat in a silence most profound—
The cat was purring about the mat,
But her mistress heard no more of that
Than if it had been a boatswain's cat;
And as for the clock the moments nicking,
The dame only gave it credit for ticking.
The bark of her dog she did not catch;
Nor yet the click of the lifted latch;
Nor yet the creak of the opening door;
Nor yet the fall of a foot on the floor—
But she saw the shadow that crept on her gown
And turned its skirt of a darker brown.

And lo! a man! a Pedlar! ay, marry,
With the little back-shop that such tradesmen carry,
Stocked with brooches, ribbons, and rings,
Spectacles, razors, and other odd things
For lad and lass, as Autolycus sings;
A chapman for goodness and cheapness of ware,
Held a fair dealer enough at a fair,
But deemed a piratical sort of invader
By him we dub the "regular trader,"
Who—luring the passengers in as they pass
By lamps, gay panels, and mouldings of brass,
And windows with only one huge pane of glass,
And his name in gilt characters, German or Roman—
If he isn't a Pedlar, at least he's a Showman!

However, in the stranger came,
And, the moment he met the eyes of the Dame,
Threw her as knowing a nod as though
He had known her fifty long years ago:
And presto! before she could utter "Jack"—

Much less "Robinson"—opened his pack—
And then from amongst his portable gear,
With even more than a Pedlar's tact,—
(Slick himself might have envied the act)—
Before she had time to be deaf, in fact—
Popped a Trumpet into her ear.
"There, Ma'am! try it!
You needn't buy it—
The last New Patent, and nothing comes nigh it
For affording the deaf, at a little expense,
The sense of hearing, and hearing of sense!
A Real Blessing—and no mistake,
Invented for poor Humanity's sake:
For what can be a greater privation
Than playing Dumby to all creation,
And only looking at conversation—
Great philosophers talking like Platos,
And Members of Parliament moral as Catos,
And your ears as dull as waxy potatoes!
Not to name the mischievous quizzers,
Sharp as knives, but double as scissors,
Who get you to answer quite by guess
Yes for No, and No for Yes."
("That's very true," says Dame Eleanor S.)

"Try it again! No harm in trying—
I'm sure you'll find it worth your buying.
A little practice—that is all—
And you'll hear a whisper, however small,
Through an Act of Parliament party-wall,—
Every syllable clear as day,
And even what people are going to say—
I wouldn't tell a lie, I wouldn't,
But my Trumpets have heard what Solomon's couldn't;
And as for Scott he promises fine,
But can he warrant his horns like mine,
Never to hear what a lady shouldn't—

Only a guinea—and can't take less."
("That's very dear," said Dame Eleanor S.)

"Dear!—Oh dear, to call it dear!
Why, it isn't a horn you buy, but an ear;
Only think, and you'll find on reflection
You're bargaining, ma'am, for the Voice of Affection;
For the language of Wisdom, and Virtue, and Truth,
And the sweet little innocent prattle of Youth:
Not to mention the striking of clocks—
Cackle of hens—crowing of cocks—
Lowing of cow, and bull, and ox—
Bleating of pretty pastoral flocks—
Murmur of waterfall over the rocks—
Every sound that Echo mocks—
Vocals, fiddles, and musical-box—
And zounds! to call such a concert dear!
But I mustn't 'swear with my horn in your ear.'
Why, in buying that Trumpet you buy all those
That Harper, or any Trumpeter, blows
At the Queen's Levees or the Lord Mayor's Shows,
At least as far as the music goes,
Including the wonderful lively sound,
Of the Guards' key-bugles all the year round;
Come—suppose we call it a pound!
Come," said the talkative Man of the Pack,
"Before I put my box on my back,
For this elegant, useful Conductor of Sound,
Come, suppose we call it a pound!

"Only a pound: it's only the price
Of hearing a concert once or twice,
It's only the fee
You might give Mr. C.
And after all not hear his advice,
But common prudence would bid you stump it;
For, not to enlarge,
It's the regular charge

At a Fancy Fair for a penny trumpet.
Lord! what's a pound to the blessing of hearing!"
("A pound's a pound," said Dame Eleanor Spearing.)

"Try it again! no harm in trying!
A pound's a pound, there's no denying;
But think what thousands and thousands of pounds
We pay for nothing but hearing sounds:
Sounds of Equity, Justice, and Law,
Parliamentary jabber and jaw,
Pious cant, and moral saw,
Hocus-pocus, and Nong-tong-paw,
And empty sounds not worth a straw;
Why, it costs a guinea, as I'm a sinner,
To hear the sounds at a public dinner!
One pound one thrown into the puddle,
To listen to Fiddle, Faddle, and Fuddle!
Not to forget the sounds we buy
From those who sell their sounds so high,
That, unless the managers pitch it strong,
To get a signora to warble a song,
You must fork out the blunt with a haymaker's prong!

"It's not the thing for me—I know it,
To crack my own trumpet up and blow it;
But it is the best, and time will show it.
There was Mrs. F.
So very deaf,
That she might have worn a percussion cap,
And been knocked on the head without hearing it snap,
Well, I sold her a horn, and the very next day
She heard from her husband at Botany Bay!
Come—eighteen shillings—that's very low,
You'll save the money as shillings go,
And I never knew so bad a lot,
By hearing whether they ring or not!

"Eighteen shillings! it's worth the price,
Supposing you're delicate-minded and nice,
To have the medical man of your choice,
Instead of the one with the strongest voice—
Who comes and asks you, how's your liver,
And where you ache, and whether you shiver,
And as to your nerves, so apt to quiver,
As if he was hailing a boat on the river!
And then, with a shout, like Pat in a riot,
Tells you to keep yourself perfectly quiet!

"Or a tradesman comes—as tradesmen will—
Short and crusty about his bill;
Of patience, indeed, a perfect scorner,
And because you're deaf and unable to pay,
Shouts whatever he has to say,
In a vulgar voice, that goes over the way,
Down the street and round the corner!
Come—speak your mind—it's 'No' or 'Yes.'"
("I've half a mind," said Dame Eleanor S.)

"Try it again—no harm in trying,
Of course you hear me, as easy as lying;
No pain at all, like a surgical trick,
To make you squall, and struggle, and kick,
Like Juno, or Rose,
Whose ear undergoes
Such horrid tugs at membrane and gristle,
For being as deaf as yourself to a whistle!

"You may go to surgical chaps if you choose,
Who will blow up your tubes like copper flues,
Or cut your tonsils right away,
As you'd shell out your almonds for Christmas Day;
And after all a matter of doubt,
Whether you ever would hear the shout
Of the little blackguards that bawl about,
'There you go with your tonsils out!'

Why I knew a deaf Welshman, who came from Glamorgan
On purpose to try a surgical spell,
And paid a guinea, and might as well
Have called a monkey into his organ!
For the Aurist only took a mug,
And poured in his ear some acoustical drug,
That, instead of curing, deafened him rather,
As Hamlet's uncle served Hamlet's father!
That's the way with your surgical gentry!
And happy your luck
If you don't get stuck
Through your liver and lights at a royal entry,
Because you never answered the sentry!

"Try it again, dear madam, try it!
Many would sell their beds to buy it.
I warrant you often wake up in the night,
Ready to shake to a jelly with fright,
And up you must get to strike a light,
And down you go, in you know what,
Whether the weather is chilly or hot,—
That's the way a cold is got,—
To see if you heard a noise or not.

"Why, bless you, a woman with organs like yours
Is hardly safe to step out of doors!
Just fancy a horse that comes full pelt,
But as quiet as if he was shod with felt,
Till he rushes against you with all his force,
And then I needn't describe of course,
While he kicks you about without remorse,
How awkward it is to be groomed by a horse!
Or a bullock comes, as mad as King Lear,
And you never dream that the brute is near,
Till he pokes his horn right into your ear,
Whether you like the thing or lump it,—
And all for want of buying a trumpet!

"I'm not a female to fret and vex,
But if I belonged to the sensitive sex,
Exposed to all sorts of indelicate sounds,
I wouldn't be deaf for a thousand pounds.
Lord! only think of chucking a copper
To Jack or Bob with a timber limb,
Who looks as if he was singing a hymn,
Instead of a song that's very improper!
Or just suppose in a public place
You see a great fellow a-pulling a face,
With his staring eyes and his mouth like an O,—
And how is a poor deaf lady to know,—
The lower orders are up to such games—
If he's calling 'Green Peas,' or calling her names?"
("They're tenpence a peck!" said the deafest of dames.)

"'Tis strange what very strong advising,
By word of mouth, or advertising,
By chalking on wall, or placarding on vans,
With fifty other different plans,
The very high pressure, in fact, of pressing,
It needs to persuade one to purchase a blessing!
Whether the soothing American Syrup,
A Safety Hat, or a Safety Stirrup,—
Infallible Pills for the human frame,
Or Rowland's O-don't-O (an ominous name)!
A Doudney's suit which the shape so hits
That it beats all others into fits;
A Mechi's razor for beards unshorn,
Or a Ghost-of-a-Whisper-Catching Horn!

"Try it again, ma'am, only try!"
Was still the voluble Pedlar's cry;
"It's a great privation, there's no dispute,
To live like the dumb unsociable brute,
And to hear no more of the pro and con,
And how Society's going on,
Than Mumbo Jumbo or Prester John,

And all for want of this sine quâ non;
Whereas, with a horn that never offends,
You may join the genteelest party that is,
And enjoy all the scandal, and gossip, and quiz,
And be certain to hear of your absent friends;—
Not that elegant ladies, in fact,
In genteel society ever detract,
Or lend a brush when a friend is blacked,—
At least as a mere malicious act,—
But only talk scandal for fear some fool
Should think they were bred at charity school.
Or, maybe, you like a little flirtation,
Which even the most Don Juanish rake
Would surely object to undertake
At the same high pitch as an altercation.
It's not for me, of course, to judge
How much a deaf lady ought to begrudge;
But half-a-guinea seems no great matter—
Letting alone more rational patter—
Only to hear a parrot chatter:
Not to mention that feathered wit,
The starling, who speaks when his tongue is slit;
The pies and jays that utter words,
And other Dicky Gossips of birds,
That talk with as much good sense and decorum
As many Beaks who belong to the Quorum.

"Try it—buy it—say ten and six,
The lowest price a miser could fix:
I don't pretend with horns of mine,
Like some in the advertising line,
To 'magnify sounds' on such marvellous scales,
That the sounds of a cod seem as big as a whale's;
But popular rumours, right or wrong,—
Charity sermons, short or long,—
Lecture, speech, concerto, or song,
All noises and voices, feeble or strong,

From the hum of a gnat to the clash of a gong,
This tube will deliver distinct and clear;
Or, supposing by chance
You wish to dance,
Why it's putting a Horn-pipe into your ear!
Try it—buy it!
Buy it—try it!
The last New Patent, and nothing comes nigh it,
For guiding sounds to their proper tunnel:
Only try till the end of June,
And if you and the trumpet are out of tune
I'll turn it gratis into a funnel!"
In short, the pedlar so beset her,—
Lord Bacon couldn't have gammoned her better,—
With flatteries plump and indirect,
And plied his tongue with such effect,—
A tongue that could almost have buttered a crumpet:
The deaf old woman bought the Trumpet.

. . . . .
. . . . .

The pedlar was gone. With the horn's assistance,
She heard his steps die away in the distance;
And then she heard the tick of the clock,
The purring of puss, and the snoring of Shock;
And she purposely dropped a pin that was little,
And heard it fall as plain as a skittle!

'Twas a wonderful horn, to be but just!
Nor meant to gather dust, must, and rust;
So in half a jiffy, or less than that,
In her scarlet cloak and her steeple-hat,
Like old Dame Trot, but without her cat,
The gossip was hunting all Tringham thorough,
As if she meant to canvass the borough,
Trumpet in hand, or up to the cavity;—
And, sure, had the horn been one of those

The wild rhinoceros wears on his nose,
It couldn't have ripped up more depravity!

Depravity! mercy shield her ears!
'Twas plain enough that her village peers
In the ways of vice were no raw beginners;
For whenever she raised the tube to her drum
Such sounds were transmitted as only come
From the very Brass Band of human sinners!
Ribald jest and blasphemous curse
(Bunyan never vented worse),
With all those weeds, not flowers, of speech
Which the Seven Dialecticians teach;
Filthy Conjunctions, and Dissolute Nouns,
And Particles picked from the kennels of towns,
With Irregular Verbs for irregular jobs,
Chiefly active in rows and mobs,
Picking Possessive Pronouns' fobs,
And Interjections as bad as a blight,
Or an Eastern blast, to the blood and the sight:
Fanciful phrases for crime and sin,
And smacking of vulgar lips where Gin,
Garlic, Tobacco, and offals go in—
A jargon so truly adapted, in fact,
To each thievish, obscene, and ferocious act,
So fit for the brute with the human shape,
Savage Baboon, or libidinous Ape,
From their ugly mouths it will certainly come
Should they ever get weary of shamming dumb!

Alas! for the Voice of Virtue and Truth,
And the sweet little innocent prattle of Youth!
The smallest urchin whose tongue could tang,
Shocked the Dame with a volley of slang,
Fit for Fagin's juvenile gang;
While the charity chap,
With his muffin cap,
His crimson coat, and his badge so garish,

Playing at dumps, or pitch in the hole,
Cursed his eyes, limbs, body and soul,
As if they did not belong to the Parish!

'Twas awful to hear, as she went along,
The wicked words of the popular song;
Or supposing she listened—as gossips will—
At a door ajar, or a window agape,
To catch the sounds they allowed to escape.
Those sounds belonged to Depravity still!
The dark allusion, or bolder brag
Of the dexterous "dodge," and the lots of "swag,"
The plundered house—or the stolen nag—
The blazing rick, or the darker crime,
That quenched the spark before its time—
The wanton speech of the wife immoral,
The noise of drunken or deadly quarrel,
With savage menace, which threatened the life,
Till the heart seemed merely a strop for the knife;
The human liver, no better than that
Which is sliced and thrown to an old woman's cat;
And the head, so useful for shaking and nodding,
To be punched into holes, like a "shocking bad hat"
That is only fit to be punched into wadding!

In short, wherever she turned the horn,
To the highly bred, or the lowly born,
The working man, who looked over the hedge,
Or the mother nursing her infant pledge.
The sober Quaker, averse to quarrels,
Or the Governess pacing the village through,
With her twelve Young Ladies, two and two,
Looking, as such young ladies do,
Trussed by Decorum and stuffed with morals—
Whether she listened to Hob or Bob,
Nob or Snob,
The Squire on his cob,
Or Trudge and his ass at a tinkering job,

To the "Saint" who expounded at "Little Zion"—
Or the "Sinner" who kept the "Golden Lion"—
The man teetotally weaned from liquor—
The Beadle, the Clerk, or the Reverend Vicar—
Nay, the very Pie in its cage of wicker—
She gathered such meanings, double or single,
That like the bell,
With muffins to sell,
Her ear was kept in a constant tingle!

But this was nought to the tales of shame,
The constant runnings of evil fame,
Foul, and dirty, and black as ink,
That her ancient cronies, with nod and wink,
Poured in her horn like slops in a sink:
While sitting in conclave, as gossips do,
With their Hyson or Howqua, black or green,
And not a little of feline spleen,
Lapped up in "Catty packages," too,
To give a zest to the sipping and supping;
For still by some invisible tether,
Scandal and Tea are linked together,
As surely as Scarification and Cupping;
Yet never since Scandal drank Bohea—
Or sloe, or whatever it happened to be,
For some grocerly thieves
Turn over new leaves,
Without much mending their lives or their tea—
No, never since cup was filled or stirred
Were such wild and horrible anecdotes heard,
As blackened their neighbours of either gender,
Especially that, which is called the Tender,
But instead of the softness we fancy therewith,
Was hardened in vice as the vice of a smith.

Women! the wretches! had soiled and marred
Whatever to womanly nature belongs;
For the marriage tie they had no regard,

Nay, sped their mates to the sexton's yard,
(Like Madame Laffarge, who with poisonous pinches
Kept cutting off her L by inches)—
And as for drinking, they drank so hard
That they drank their flat-irons, pokers, and tongs!

The men—they fought and gambled at fairs;
And poached—and didn't respect grey hairs—
Stole linen, money, plate, poultry, and corses;
And broke in houses as well as horses;
Unfolded folds to kill their own mutton,—
And would their own mothers and wives for a button:
But not to repeat the deeds they did,
Backsliding in spite of all moral skid,
If all were true that fell from the tongue,
There was not a villager, old or young,
But deserved to be whipped, imprisoned, or hung,
Or sent on those travels which nobody hurries,
To publish at Colburn's, or Longmans', or Murray's.

Meanwhile the Trumpet, con amore,
Transmitted each vile diabolical story;
And gave the least whisper of slips and falls,
As that Gallery does in the Dome of St. Paul's,
Which, as all the world knows, by practice or print,
Is famous for making the most of a hint.
Not a murmur of shame,
Or buzz of blame,
Not a flying report that flew at a name,
Not a plausible gloss, or significant note,
Not a word in the scandalous circles afloat,
Of a beam in the eye, or diminutive mote,
But vortex-like that tube of tin
Sucked the censorious particle in;
And, truth to tell, for as willing an organ
As ever listened to serpent's hiss,
Nor took the viperous sound amiss,
On the snaky head of an ancient Gorgon!

The Dame, it is true, would mutter "shocking!"
And give her head a sorrowful rocking,
And make a clucking with palate and tongue,
Like the call of Partlet to gather her young,
A sound, when human, that always proclaims
At least a thousand pities and shames;
But still the darker the tale of sin,
Like certain folks, when calamities burst,
Who find a comfort in "hearing the worst,"
The farther she poked the Trumpet in.
Nay, worse, whatever she heard she spread
East and West, and North and South,
Like the ball which, according to Captain Z.,
Went in at his ear, and came out at his mouth.
What wonder between the Horn and the Dame,
Such mischief was made wherever they came,
That the parish of Tringham was all in a flame!

For although it required such loud discharges,
Such peals of thunder as rumbled at Lear,
To turn the smallest of table-beer,
A little whisper breathed into the ear
Will sour a temper "as sour as varges."
In fact such very ill blood there grew,
From this private circulation of stories,
That the nearest neighbours the village through,
Looked at each other as yellow and blue,
As any electioneering crew
Wearing the colours of Whigs and Tories.
Ah! well the Poet said, in sooth,
That "whispering tongues can poison Truth,"—
Yes, like a dose of oxalic acid,
Wrench and convulse poor Peace, the placid,
And rack dear Love with internal fuel,
Like arsenic pastry, or what is as cruel,
Sugar of lead, that sweetens gruel,—
At least such torments began to wring 'em

From the very morn
When that mischievous Horn
Caught the whisper of tongues in Tringham.

The Social Clubs dissolved in huffs,
And the Sons of Harmony came to cuffs,
While feuds arose and family quarrels,
That discomposed the mechanics of morals,
For screws were loose between brother and brother,
While sisters fastened their nails on each other;
Such wrangles, and jangles, and miff, and tiff,
And spar, and jar—and breezes as stiff
As ever upset a friendship—or skiff!
The plighted lovers who used to walk,
Refused to meet, and declined to talk:
And wished for two moons to reflect the sun,
That they mightn't look together on one:
While wedded affection ran so low,
That the oldest John Anderson snubbed his Jo—
And instead of the toddle adown the hill,
Hand in hand,
As the song has planned,
Scratched her, penniless, out of his will!
In short, to describe what came to pass
In a true, though somewhat theatrical way,
Instead of "Love in a Village"—alas!
The piece they performed was "The Devil to Pay!"

However, as secrets are brought to light,
And mischief comes home like chickens at night;
And rivers are tracked throughout their course,
And forgeries traced to their proper source;—
And the sow that ought
By the ear is caught,—
And the sin to the sinful door is brought;
And the cat at last escapes from the bag—
And the saddle is placed on the proper nag—
And the fog blows off, and the key is found—

And the faulty scent is picked out by the hound—
And the fact turns up like a worm from the ground—
And the matter gets wind to waft it about;
And a hint goes abroad, and the murder is out—
And a riddle is guessed—and the puzzle is known—
So the Truth was sniffed, and the Trumpet was blown!

. . . . .

'Tis a day in November—a day of fog—
But the Tringham people are all agog!
Fathers, Mothers, and Mothers' Sons,—
With sticks, and staves, and swords, and guns,—
As if in pursuit of a rabid dog;
But their voices—raised to the highest pitch—
Declare that the game is "a Witch!—a Witch!"

Over the Green and along by the George—
Past the Stocks and the Church, and the Forge,
And round the Pound, and skirting the Pond,
Till they come to the whitewashed cottage beyond,
And there at the door they muster and cluster,
And thump, and kick, and bellow, and bluster—
Enough to put Old Nick in a fluster!
A noise, indeed, so loud and long,
And mixed with expressions so very strong,
That supposing, according to popular fame,
"Wise Woman" and Witch to be the same,
No hag with a broom would unwisely stop,
But up and away through the chimney-top;
Whereas, the moment they burst the door,
Planted fast on her sanded floor,
With her trumpet up to her organ of hearing,
Lo and behold!—Dame Eleanor Spearing!

Oh! then rises the fearful shout—
Bawled and screamed, and bandied about—
"Seize her!—Drag the old Jezebel out!"
While the Beadle—the foremost of all the band,

Snatches the Horn from her trembling hand—
And after a pause of doubt and fear,
Puts it up to his sharpest ear.
"Now silence—silence—one and all!"
For the Clerk is quoting from Holy Paul!
But before he rehearses
A couple of verses,
The Beadle lets the Trumpet fall!
For instead of the words so pious and humble,
He hears a supernatural grumble.

Enough, enough! and more than enough;—
Twenty impatient hands and rough,
By arm and leg, and neck and scruff,
Apron, 'kerchief, gown of stuff—
Cap and pinner, sleeve and cuff—
Are clutching the Witch wherever they can,
With the spite of woman and fury of man;
And then—but first they kill her cat,
And murder her dog on the very mat—
And crush the infernal Trumpet flat;—
And then they hurry her through the door
She never, never will enter more!

Away! away! down the dusty lane
They pull her and haul her, with might and main;
And happy the hawbuck, Tom or Harry,
Dandy or Sandy, Jerry or Larry,
Who happens to get "a leg to carry!"
And happy the foot that can give her a kick,
And happy the hand that can find a brick—
And happy the fingers that hold a stick—
Knife to cut, or pin to prick—
And happy the boy who can lend her a lick;—
Nay, happy the urchin—Charity-bred,—
Who can shy very nigh to her wicked old head!

Alas! to think how people's creeds
Are contradicted by people's deeds!
But though the wishes that Witches utter
Can play the most diabolical rigs—
Send styes in the eye—and measle the pigs—
Grease horses' heels—and spoil the butter;
Smut and mildew the corn on the stalk—
And turn new milk to water and chalk,—
Blight apples—and give the chickens the pip—
And cramp the stomach—and cripple the hip—
And waste the body—and addle the eggs—
And give a baby bandy legs;
Though in common belief a Witch's curse
Involves all these horrible things and worse—
As ignorant bumpkins all profess,
No bumpkin makes a poke the less
At the back or ribs of old Eleanor S.!
As if she were only a sack of barley!
Or gives her credit for greater might
Than the Powers of Darkness confer at night
On that other old woman, the parish Charley!

Ay, now's the time for a Witch to call
On her imps and sucklings one and all—
Newes, Pyewacket, or Peck in the Crown,
(As Matthew Hopkins has handed them down)
Dick, and Willet, and Sugar-and-Sack,
Greedy Grizel, Jarmara the Black,
Vinegar Tom, and the rest of the pack—
Ay, now's the nick for her friend Old Harry
To come "with his tail," like the bold Glengarry,
And drive her foes from their savage job
As a mad black bullock would scatter a mob:—
But no such matter is down in the bond;
And spite of her cries that never cease,
But scare the ducks and astonish the geese,
The dame is dragged to the fatal pond!

And now they come to the water's brim—
And in they bundle her—sink or swim;
Though it's twenty to one that the wretch must drown,
With twenty sticks to hold her down;
Including the help to the self-same end,
Which a travelling Pedlar stops to lend.
A Pedlar!—Yes!—The same!—the same!
Who sold the Horn to the drowning Dame!
And now is foremost amid the stir,
With a token only revealed to her;
A token that makes her shudder and shriek,
And point with her finger, and strive to speak—
But before she can utter the name of the Devil,
Her head is under the water level!

Moral.

There are folks about town—to name no names—
Who much resemble the deafest of Dames!
And over their tea, and muffins, and crumpets,
Circulate many a scandalous word,
And whisper tales they could only have heard
Through some such Diabolical Trumpets!

By Thomas Hood

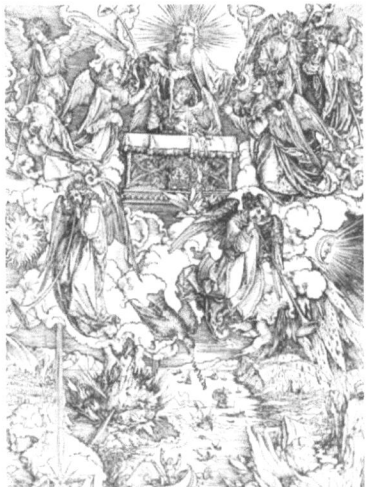

The Seven Trumpets Are Given To The Angels--Albrecht Durer--Northern Renaissance

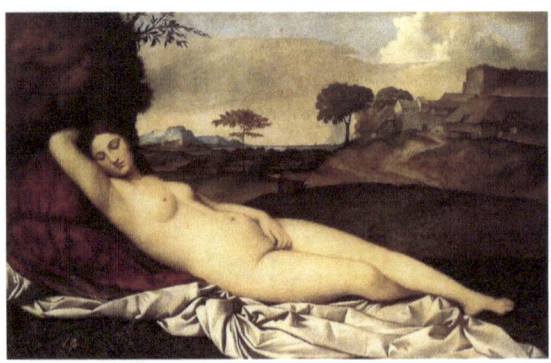

The Sleeping Venus (Venere dormente)--Giorgione--High Renaissance

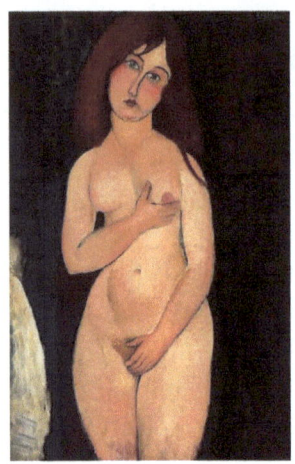

Venus (Standing Nude)--Amedeo Modigliani—1917--Expressionism

A Hymn To Venus

O Venus, beauty of the skies,
To whom a thousand temples rise,
Gaily false in gentle smiles,
Full of love-perplexing wiles;
O goddess, from my heart remove
The wasting cares and pains of love.

If ever thou hast kindly heard
A song in soft distress preferred,
Propitious to my tuneful vow,
A gentle goddess, hear me now.
Descend, thou bright immortal guest,
In all thy radiant charms confessed.

Thou once didst leave almighty Jove
And all the golden roofs above:
The car thy wanton sparrows drew,
Hovering in air they lightly flew;
As to my bower they winged their way
I saw their quivering pinions play.

The birds dismissed (while you remain)
Bore back their empty car again:
Then you, with looks divinely mild,
In every heavenly feature smiled,
And asked what new complaints I made,
And why I called you to my aid?

What frenzy in my bosom raged,
And by what cure to be assuaged?
What gentle youth I would allure,
Whom in my artful toils secure?
Who does thy tender heart subdue,
Tell me, my Sappho, tell me who?

Though now he shuns thy longing arms,
He soon shall court thy slighted charms;
Though now thy offerings he despise,
He soon to thee shall sacrifice;
Though now he freezes, he soon shall burn,
And be thy victim in his turn.

Celestial visitant, once more
Thy needful presence I implore.
In pity come, and ease my grief,
Bring my distempered soul relief,
Favour thy suppliant's hidden fires,
And give me all my heart desires.

Sappho

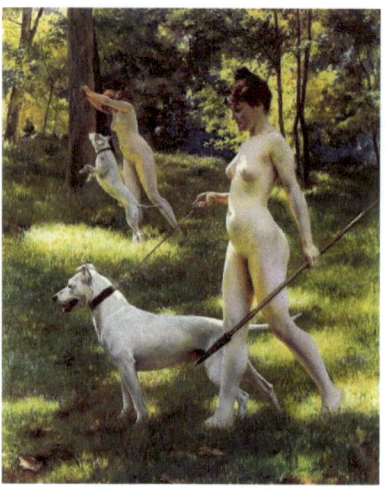

Nymphs Hunting--Julius LeBlanc Stewart—1898--Academicism

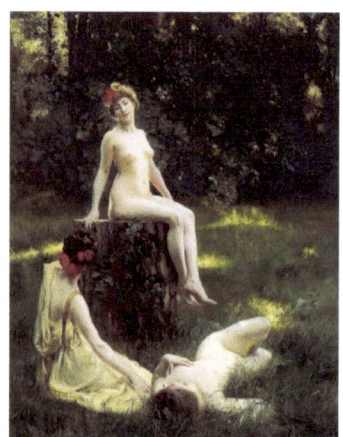

The Glade--Julius LeBlanc Stewart—1900--Academicism

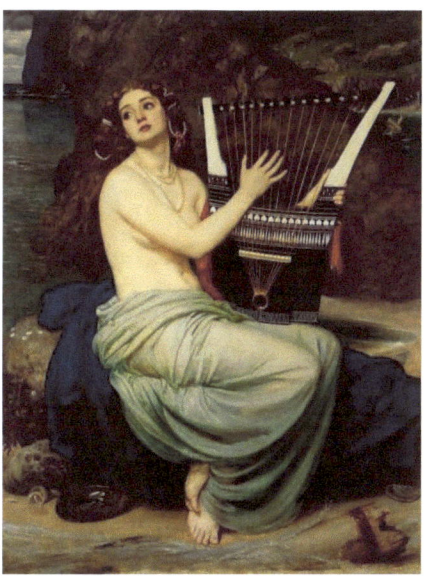

The Siren--Sir Edward John Poynter--1864

For thy last dear one! Lie in her embrace —
Till shines a new star on thy raptured eyes!
Fonder of maids thou art, I trow, than she.
The ghost who nightly steal young girls, to be
In Hades of her woeful company.
This is my fair girl-garden: sweet they grow —
Rose, violet, asphodel and lily's snow;
And which the sweetest is, I do not know;
For rosy arms and starry eyes are there.
Honey-sweet voices and cheeks passing fair.
And these shall men, I ween, remember long;
For these shall bloom for ever in my song.

Sappho

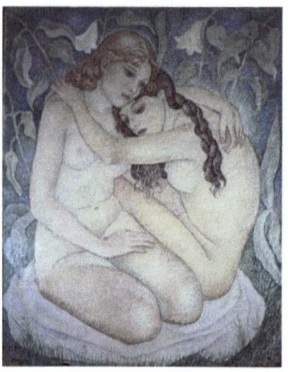

Playing--Marevna (Marie Vorobieff)--Pointillism

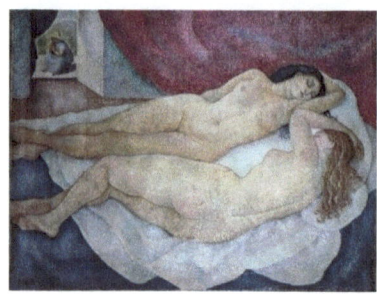

Marevna (Marie Vorobieff)

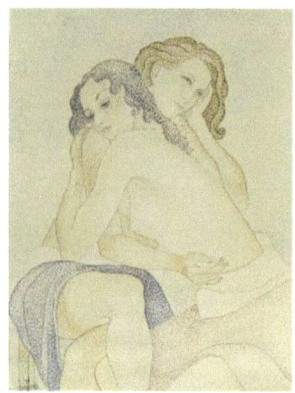

Marevna (Marie Vorobieff)

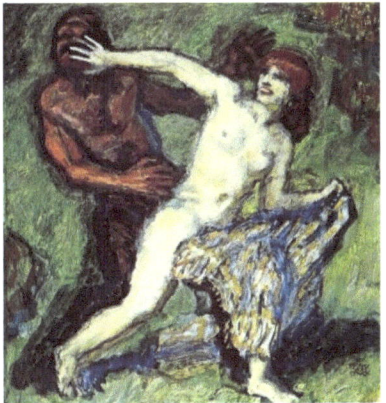

Fishing Game (Faun And Nymph)--Franz Stuck--c.1904--Symbolism

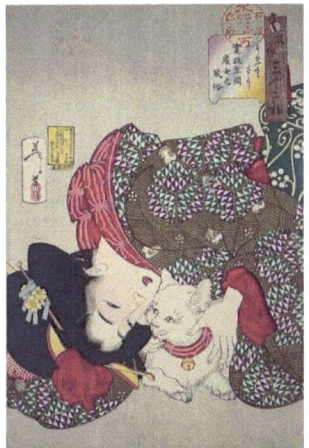

A Young Woman From Kansei Period Playing With Her Cat--Tsukioka Yoshitoshi—1888--Ukiyo-e

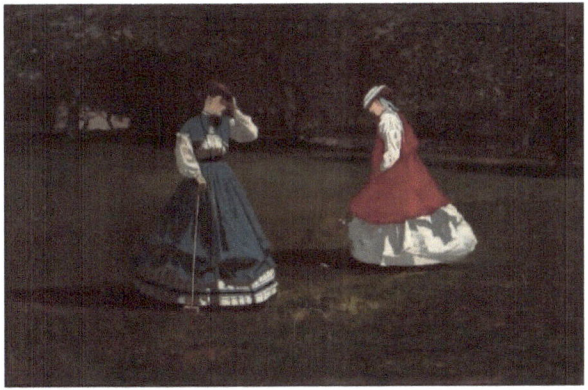

Game Of Croquet--Winslow Homer--Realism

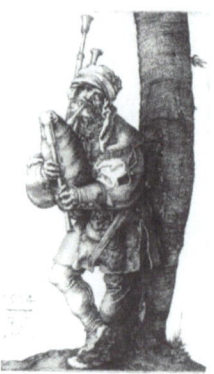

Bagpipes Players--Albrecht Durer—1514--Northern Renaissance

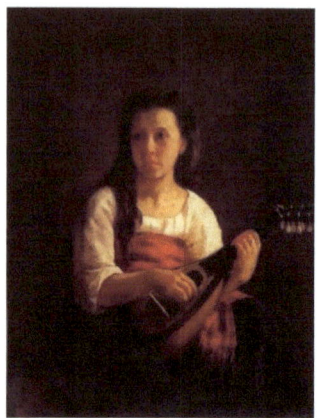

The Mandolin Player--Mary Cassatt--1872--Realism

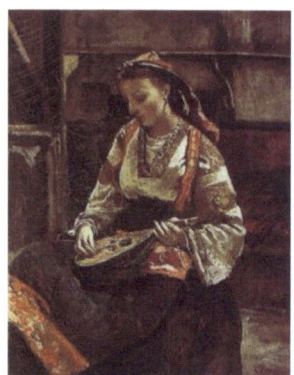

Bind me -- I still can sing

Bind me -- I still can sing --

Banish -- my mandolin

Strikes true within --

Slay -- and my Soul shall rise

Chanting to Paradise --

Still thine.

Emily Dickinson

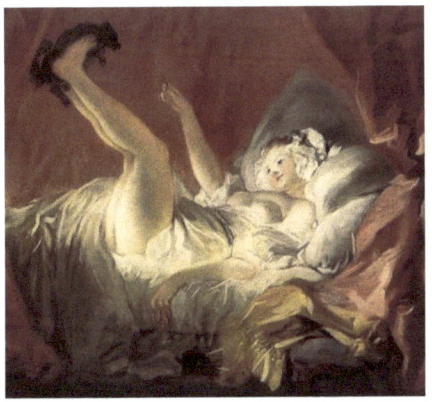

Young Woman Playing With A Dog--Jean-Honore Fragonard--Rococo

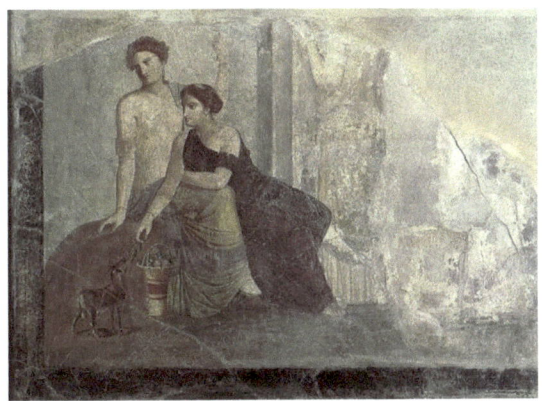

Women playing with a goat, Roman city of Pompeii (mural painting)

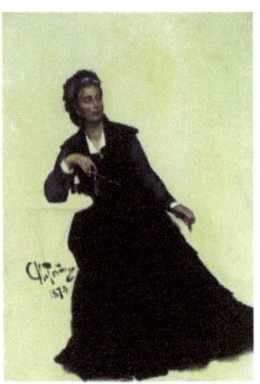

Woman Playing With Umbrella (Дама, играющая зонтиком)--Ilya Repin—1874--Realism

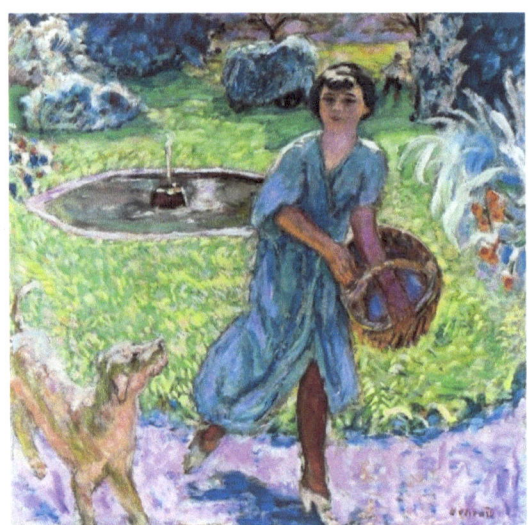

Girl Playing With A Dog (Vivette Terrasse)--Pierre Bonnard—1913--Post-Impressionism

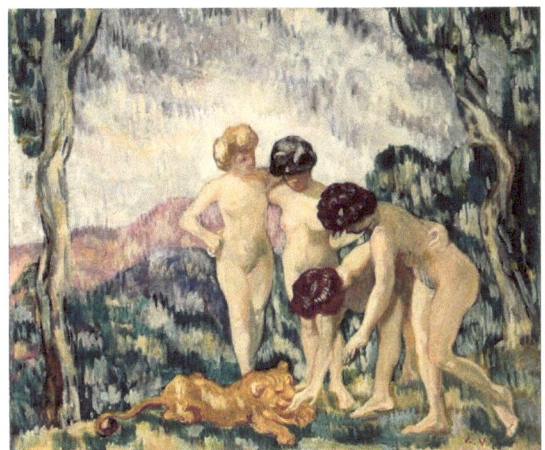

Young Girls Playing With A Lion Cub--Louis Valtat--Fauvism

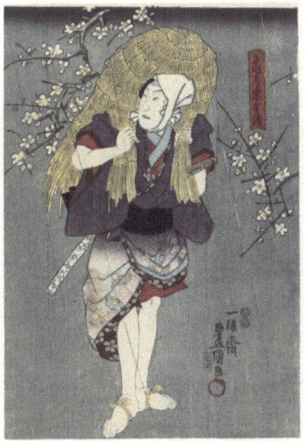

The Actor Playing A Farmer--Utagawa Kunisada--Ukiyo-e--yakusha-e

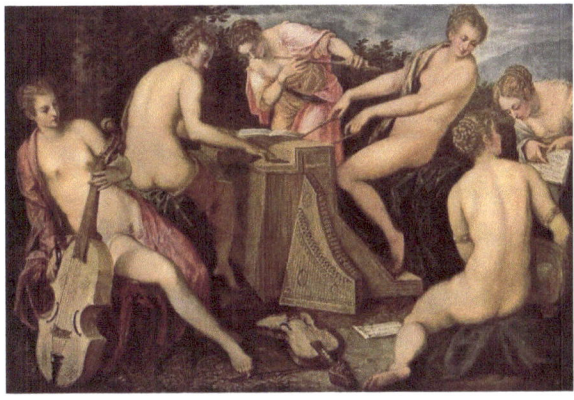

Women Playing Instruments--Tintoretto--Mannerism

www.ingramcontent.com/pod-product-compliance
Lightning Source LLC
Chambersburg PA
CBHW051205220526
45473CB00003B/909

References

1- B. Arivazhagan, R. Prabhu, S.k. Albert, M. Kamaraj and S. Sundaresan, " Microstructure and Mechanical Properties of 9Cr-1Mo Steel Weld Fusion Zones as a Function of Weld Metal Composition ", ASM International, July 2008.

2- A. Czyrska, A. Lipiec and P. J Ennis, " Modified 9% Cr Steels for Advanced Power Generation: Microstructure and Properties ", Journal of Achievements in Materials and Manufacturing Engineering, Vol. 19, Issue 2, December, 2006.

3- H.G. Kang and S. Y. Bae, " Fatigue Crack Growth Rate in Low ΔK Range According to The Microstructure and Temperature in P122 Alloy Steel ", Graduate School of Mechanical Engineering, Sungkyunkwan University, Korea, 2006.

4- S. Kjaer and J. Bugge, " Europeans Still Aiming for 700 °C Steam ", Elsam Engineering, Fredericia, Denmark, MPS Review Supercritical PF Technology, November 2004.

5- ASME Boiler and Pressure Vessel Code, "Ferrous Materials Specifications ", Section II, 2007 addenda 2008.

6- I. A. Shibli, " Failures of P91 Steel at The West Burton Plant in England Raise Concerns About The Long Term Behavior of The Advanced Steel ", European Technology Development, UK, http://www.ommi.co.uk/etd/ETD-EPRI-%20P91%20Failures.pdf.

7- H. Heuser and C. Jochum, " Alloy Design for Similar and Dissimilar Welding and Their Behaviors ", Bőhler Thyssen Schweisstechnik Deutschland GmbH, Germany, 2005.

8- M. Staubli, R.. Hanus, J. Stief, K-H. Mayer and T-U.Kern, " The European Efforts in Development of New High Temperature Casing Materials – COST536 ", European Cooperation in Science and Technology, acction of COST 536, http://www.cost.esf.org/domains_actions/mpns/Actions/ACCEPT., Google search, January 2010.

9- K. Savolalianen, J. Mononen, R. Ilola, and H. Hanninen, " Materials Selection for High Temperature Applications ", Helsinki University of Technology, Department of Mechanical Engineering, Laboratory of Engineering Materials, 2005.

10- R.W. Hertzberg, " Deformation and Fracture Mechanics of Engineering Materials", Wiley, Materials Science emphasis, 4th edition, 1996.

11- R. Viswanathan, " Damage Mechanisms and Life Assessment of High-Temperature Components ", ASM International, Ohio, USA, 1989

12- R. David Thomas, " Material Requirments for Service Conditions ", ASM Hand Book, Welding, Brazing and Soldering, Vol. 6, 3^d edition, 1995.

13- I. Von Hagen and W. Bendick, " Creep Resistant Ferritic Steels for Power Plants ", International Symposium on Niobium 2001; Orlando, FL; USA; 2-5 Dec. 2001. pp. 753-776. 2002.

14- G. Kalwa, " State of the Development and Application Techniques of the Steel X20CrMoV12-1", Nuclear Engineering and Design, 84 (1985), 87-95.

15- R. Blum et al., "Newly Developed High-Temperature Ferritic-Martensitic Steels from USA, Japan, and Europe", VGB Kraftwerkstechnik (English Issue), pp 553-563, 1994.

16- V.K. Sikka, C.T. Ward, and K.C. Thomas, " Modified 9Cr-1Mo Steel – An Improved Alloy for Steam Generator Application", (Paper presented at conference Ferritic Steels for High- Temperature Applications, Warren, Pa., 6-8 October 1981).

17- D.A. Canonico, "Thick-Walled Pressure Vessels for Energy Systems", Technical Program and Data Package for Use of Modified 9Cr-1Mo Steel, ASME Sect. I and VIII, April 1982.

18- R. Foret, B. Zlamal, and J. Sopousek, " Structural Stability of Dissimilar Weld between Two Cr-Mo-V Steels ", Supplement to The Welding Jornal, American Welding Society and the Welding Research Council, October 2006.

19- R. Viswanathan and W. T. Bakker, " Materials for Boilers in Ultra Supercritical Power Plants ", International Joint Power Generation Conference, Florida, July 2000.

20- TWI Services, " New 9-13%Cr weld Metal ", Power Industry, www.twi.co.uk/content/power_newweldmet.html, 2005.

21- F. Masuyama, " History of Power Plants and Progress in Heat Resistant Steels", ISIJ International, Vol. 41 (2001), No. 6, pp. 612–625, December 2000.

22- D. Kopeliovich, " Effect of Alloying elements on Steel Properties", http://www.substech.com/dokuwiki/doku.php?id=effect_of_alloying_elements_on_steel_properties, September 2009.

23- Key to metal, "Influence of Alloying Elements on Steel Microstructure", steel.keytometals.com/articles/art50.htm, 2009.

24- Y.Murata, M. Kamyia, T. Kunieda, A. M. AbdEl-Daiem, T. Koyama, M. Morinaga, and R. Hashizume, " Dependence of Solvus Temperature of the Laves Phase on (Mo+W+Re) Contents in High Ferritic Steels", ISIJ International, Vol. 45, No.1, pp 101 106 , 2005,http://www.jstage.jst.go.jp/article/isijinternational/45/1/101/_pdf,

25- K. Savolainen, J. Mononen, R. Ilola, H. Hanninen, " Material Selection for High Temperature Application", Helsinki University of Technology, Department of Mechanical Engineering, Laboratory of Engineering Materials, 2005.

26- K. Yoshikawa, A. Iseda, M. Yano, F. Masuyama, T. Daikoku and H. Haneda: 1st Int. Conf. Improved Coal-Fired Power Plants, Palo Alto, CA, (1986).

27- Y. Tsuda, R. Ishii, M. Yamada, T. Azuma, Y. Tanaka and Y. Ikeda: Proc. Int. Conf. Power Engineering–'97, Vol. 2, JSME, Tokyo, (1997), 131.

28- T. Fujita, " Thermal Nuclear Power" , 42 (1991), 1485.

29- T. Shinoda and R. Tanaka: Bull. Jpn. Inst. Met., 11 (1972), 180.

30- Y. Sawaragi, K. Ogawa, S. Kato, A. Natori and S. Hirano: Sumitomo Search, 48 (1992), 50.

31- S. Ohta: Tetsu-to-Hagané, 80 (1996), N227.

32- M. Yoshino, Y. Mishima, Y. TODA, H. Kushima and K. SAWADA, " Phase Equilibrium between Austenite and MX Carbonitrides in a 9Cr-1Mo-V-Nb Steel ", ISIJ International, Vol.45, No.1, pp. 107-115, 2005

33- P. J. Ennis and A Czyrska-Filemonowicz, " Recent Advances in Creep Resistant Steels for Power Plant Applications ", OMMI (Vol 1, No.1) April 2002.

34- A. Di Gianfrancesco, L. Cipolla, F. Cirilli, C. Sviluppo, G. Cumino, S. Caminada and T. Dalmine, " Microstructural Stability and Creep Data Assessment of Tenaris Grades 91 and 911 ", Italy, 2005.

35- J. Pasternak, " Structural Stability of New Creep Resisting Steel Grades With 9 and 12% Cr Contents Applied in Power Generation Sector in Industrial Condition", Boiler Engineering Factory RAFAKO, http://www.msm.cam.ac.uk/phasetrans/2005/LINK/77.pdf, 2005.

36- F. Vodopivec, "Microstructural Stability of 9-12 % Chromium Steels, COST 5001 Report Contract No. 94-0076-CZ (DG 12CSMS).

37- F. Vodopivec, M. Jenko, and J. Vojvodic-Tuma, " Stability of MC Carbide Particles Size in Creep Resisting Steels ", February 2006.

38- J. Hald and L. Corcakova, " Precipitate Stability in Creep Resistant Ferritic Steels- Experimental Investigations and Modeling ", ISJI International, Vol. 43 (2003), No.3, pp. 420-427.

39- J. Hald, "Creep Resistant 9-12% Cr Steels- Long- Term Testing, Microstracture Stability and Development Potentials ", Elsam/Energy E2/IPL-MPT TU Denmark, 2005.

40- Fujio Abe, " High performance creep Resistantg Steels for 21St Century Power Plants", National Institute of Material Science, Nov. 2005. www.msm.cam.ac.uk/phasetrans/2005/LINK/84.pdf

41- T. Ishitsuka and H. Mimura, " Development of 18Cr-9Ni-W-Nb-V-N Austenitic Stainless Steel Tube for Thermal Power Boilers ", JSME International Journal, Vol. 45, No.1, 2002.

42- Milton Ohring, " Engineering Material Science ", Department of Material Science and Engineering ", Stevence Institute of Technology, Hoboken, New Jersey, Dec.1995.

43- R. A. Higgins, " Materials for Engineers and Technicians ", Fourth Edition, 2006.

44- Myer Kutz, " Hand Book of Materials Selection ",2002 by John Wiley & Sons, New York, 2002

45- Michael G. Jenkins, " Mechanics of Materials Laboratory ", Department of Mechanical Engineering University of Washington Seattle, Washington, Jan 2001, Course website: http://swhite.me.washington.edu/~jenkinsm/me354/

46- William F. Hosford, " Mechanical Behavior of Materials ", Cambridge University Press, 2005.

47- Jan Hilkes and Volker Gross, " Welding CrMo Steels for Power Generation and Petrochemical Applications ", IIW Conference, Singapore, July 2009.

48- European Creep Collaborative Committee's, " Advanced Creep Data For Plant Design and Life Extension ", One day Seminar, September 2003.

49- American Society of Mechanical Engineering, " ASME Boiler and Pressure Vessel code 2007, add. 2009 ", July 2009.

50- J E Oakey, Cranfield University, L W Pinder, Powergen UK UK plc, R Vanstone and M Henderson, ALSTOM Power , S Osgerby, National Physical Laboratory, " Review of Status of Advanced Materials for Power Generation ", Report No. COAL R224 DTI/Pub URN 02/1509.

51- Ehlers R J and Quadakkers W J, " Oxidation von Ferritischen 9-12% Cr-Staehlen in wasserdampfhaltigen Atmosphaeren bei 550 bis 650°C, Doctor thesis published as report of the ResearchCentre Juelich Juel-3883, ISSN 0944-2952, June 2001.

52- Quadakkers W J and Ennis P J, " The Oxidation Behavior of Ferritic and Austenitic Steels in Simulated Power plant Service Environments", in Materials for Advanced Power Engineering 1998, ed J.Lecomte-Beckers, F.Schubert, P.J.Ennis, ISBN 389336 228-2, Forschungs zentrum.

53- P J Ennis[1] and A Czyrska-Filemonowicz[2], " Recent Advances in Creep Resistant Steels for Power Plant Applications ", OMMI (Vol 1, No.1) April 2002.

54- ASM Metals Handbook, ninth edition, volume 6, "Welding, Brazing, and Soldering", p248-250.

55- M. L. Santella, R. W. Swindeman, R. W. Reed , and J. M. Tanzosh , " Martensitic transformation, microsegregation, and creep strength 9 Cr-1Mo-V steel weld metal ", http://www.ornl.gov/~webworks/cppr/y2001/pres/113751.pdf, Oak Ridge National Laboratory, 2001.

56- Beres, L., Balogh, A., and Irmer, W. "Welding of martensitic creep-resistant steels", 2001, Welding Journal 80(8): 191-s to 195-s.

57- MPA Stuttgart, " Investigations on the Integrity of repair welds", Germany; Co-operating partners; ENEL Produzione, Italy, Bristol University, UK, European Technology Dev. (ETD), UK, Siempelkamp Prüf- und Gutachterges., Dresden, Germany, JRC Petten, Netherlands, CEA, Saclay, France, MT Integridade, Portugal, Laborelec, Belgium;, EU project GRD1-1999-10886.

58- David Allen, " Avoidance of Premature Weld Failure by ' Type IV ' Cracking ", Cleaner Fossil Fuels R & D Program, Harwell International Business Center, July 2005.

59- K. Maile, A. Klenk, M. Bauer and E. Roos, " Consideration of Weld Behavior in Design of High Temperature Components ", Fifth International conference on advances in material Technology for Fossil Power Plants, September 2007.

60- Schubert, J., A. Klenk and K. Maile: Determination of weld strength factors for the creep rupture strength of welded joints. International Conference on Creep and Fracture in High Temperature Components – Design and Life Assessment Issues, European Creep Collaborative Committee (ECCC), IOM London, 12-14 September 2005.

61- AVIF Forschungsvorhaben A 196, Längsnahtgeschweißte Rohre, Abschlussbericht, MPA Universität Stuttgart, 2006,

62- "Creep and Stress rupture", http://www.materialsengineer.c om/CA-Creep-Stress-Rupture.htm .

63- ASM Metals Handbook, ninth edition, vol. 8, Mechanical Testing, p. 318-322.

64- Boris Ule, Monika Jenko, Roman Sturm "Accelerated small-punch creep testing" Materiali in Tehnologije 36 (2002) 6.

65- P. Jung a, A. Hishinuma b, G.E. Lucas c, H. Ullmaier "Recommendation of miniaturized techniques for mechanical testing of fusion materials in an intense neutron source" Journal of Nuclear Materials 232 (1996), pp. 186-205.

66- Michael F Ashby and David R H Jones, "Engineering Materials 1, An Introduction to their Properties and Applications" second edition, volume 1, ISBN 0 7506 30817, Department of Engineering, University of Cambridge, UK, p 185 202.

67- ECCC Recommendations," Data Acceptability Criteria and Data Generation: Creep Data For Welds ", Vol. 3, Part II, Issue 3, 2005.

68- T.Igari, F.Kawashima, T.Tokiyoshi, N.Nishimura and N.Tada, " Microscopic Damage Analysis of Welded Joints Under Type III and Type IV Creep Failure", OMMI (Vol.3, Issue 3) December 2004.

69- Masaaki Tabuchi, Masayuki Kondo, Kiyoshi Kubo and Shaju K. Albert, " Improvement of Type IV Creep Cracking Resistance of 9Cr Heat Resisting Steels By Boron Addition", National Institute for Materials Science (NIMS), Japan, OMMI (Vol.3, Issue 3) December 2004.

70- Evans and Wilshire, " Introduction to Creep" , The Institute of Materials, London, PP 1-77, 1993.

71- Bernasconi, and Piatti, " Creep Engineering Materials and Structures", Applied Science Publisher, 1978.

72- K. Coleman, "Guideline for Welding Creep Strength-Enhanced Ferritic Alloys", Electrical Power Research Institute ERPI , Technical Update, 1012748, March 2007.

73- Kent K. Colleman and W.F. Newwll JR, " P91 and Beyond, Welding the New-generation Cr-Mo Alloys for High-Temperature Service ", Electric Power Research Institute, Charlotte, N.C. W. F, WELDING JOURNAL, http://files.aws.org/wj/2007/wj0807-29.pdf, 2007.

74- American Society of Mechanical Engineering, "ASME Boiler and Pressure Vessel code 2007, add. 2009, Section II, Part A ", July 2009.

75- American Society of Mechanical Engineering, "Power Piping Code ASME B31.1", 2007.

76- American Society for Testing and Material, " ASTM G36-94, Standard practice for evaluating stress-corrosion- cracking resistance of metals and alloys in a boiling magnesium chloride solution", 2006.

77- American Society for Testing and Material, " ASTM G30-97, Standard practice for making and using U-bend stress-corrosion test specimens", 2009.

78- J. M. Race and H. K. D. H Bhadishia, " Precipitation sequence during decarburization of Cr-Mo steel", Institute of Materials, University of Cambridge, 1992.

79- J. Pilling and N. Ridley, Metall. Trans., 1982, 13A, 557-563.

80- C. Panait1, W. Bendick3, A. Fuchsmann, A.-F. Gourgues-Lorenzon, J. Besson, "Study of the microstructure of the Grade 91 steel after more than 100,000h of creep exposure at 600°C", International Journal of Pressure Vessels and Piping 87 (2010) 326-335.

81- Kaneko K., Matsumura S., Sadakata A., Fujita K., Moon W. –J., Ozaki S., Nishimura N., Tomokyio Y., " Characterization of carbides at different boundaries of 9Cr-steel", Materials Science and Engineering A374 (2004) 82-89.

82- J. Hald and L. Korcakova, "Precipitate Stability in Creep Resistant Ferritic Steels– Experimental Investigations and Modeling", ISIJ International, Vol. 43 (2003), No. 3, pp. 420–427.

83- A. Aghajani, " Evolution of Microstructure During Long-Term Creep of Tempered Martensite Ferritic Steel", Aus Tahran, Iran, 2009.

84- R. W. Balluffi, M. Cohen, and B. L. Averbach: Trans. ASM, 1951, 43, 497-526.

85- Hradec nad Moravicí, "Creep Behaviour And Microstructure Of Aheterogeneous P23/P91 Weld", Vlastimil Vodárek Lucie Strílková Zdenek Kubon MATERIÁLOVÝ A METALURGICKÝ VÝZKUM s.r.o., Pohranicní 31, 706 02 Ostrava-Vítkovice, CR, vlastimil.vodarek@mmvyzkum.cz), METAL- 2009.

86- Sopoušek J.; Foret R.; Jan V., "Simulation of Dissimilar Weld Joints of Steel P91", Science and Technology of Welding & Joining, Vol. 9, pp. 59-64, 2004.

87- Dejun Li, Kenji Shinozaki, Hidemasa Harada and Kenji Ohishi, "Investigation of precipitation behavior in a weld deposit of 11Cr-2W ferritic steel", metallurgical and materials transactions, volume 36, number 1 (2005).

88- Castolin Eutectic, "Welding and Coating Metallurgy", 1999, www.castolin.com/sites/.../Welding_Coating.pdf

89- B. Arivazhagan, G. Srinivasan, S.K. Albert, A.K. Bhaduri, " A Study on Influence of Heat input Variation on Microstructure of Reduced Activation Ferritic Martensitic Steel Weld Metal Produced by GTAW Process", Fusion Engineering and Design, Vol. 86, pp. 192–197, 2011.

90- V.K. Sikka, C.T. Ward, and K.C. Thomas: Proc. Int. Conf. on Ferritic Steels for High Temperature Applications, A.K. Khare, ed., ASM, Metals Park, OH, 1983, pp. 65-84.

91- Wendell B. Jones: Proc. Int. Conf. on Ferritic Steels for High Temperature Applications, A.K. Khare, ed., ASM, Metals Park, OH, 1983, pp.116-30.

92- Wendell B. Jones, C.R. Hills, and D.H. Polonis: Metall. Trans. A, 1991, vol. 22A, pp. 1049-58.

93- C. Panait1, W. Bendick3, A. Fuchsmann, A.-F. Gourgues-Lorenzon, J. Besson, "Study of the microstructure of the Grade 91 steel after more than 100,000h of creep exposure at 600°C", International Journal of Pressure Vessels and Piping 87 (2010) 326-335.

94- H.K.D.H. Bhadeshia, " Design of Ferritic creep resistant steel" ISIJ international, Vol.41 (2001), No.6 ,pp .626-640.

95- KlasWeman, "Welding processes handbook", New York, 2003: CRC Press LLC. ISBN 0-8493-1773-8.

96- P. Scherrer, "Bestimmung der Grösse und der inneren Struktur von Kolloidteilchen mittels Röntgenstrahlen," Nachr. Ges. Wiss. Göttingen 26 (1918) pp 98-100.

97- J.I. Langford and A.J.C. Wilson, "Scherrer after Sixty Years: A Survey and Some New Results in the Determination of Crystallite Size," J. Appl. Cryst. 11 (1978) pp 102-113.

98- Scott A Speakman, "Estimating Crystallite Size Using XRD", Ph.D., MIT Center for Materials Science and Engineering (CMSE), speakman@mit.edu, http://prism.mit.edu/xray.

99- A. Di Gianfrancesco, L. Cipolla, F. Cirilli, C. Sviluppo, G. Cumino, S. Caminada and T. Dalmine, " Microstructural Stability and Creep Data Assessment of Tenaris Grades 91 and 911 ", Italy, 2005.

100- G.Guntz, M. Julien, G. Kottmann, F. Pellicani, A.Pouilly, J. C.Vaillant, "The T91 book",Vallourec Industries, France, 1990.

101- K Maile, "Evaluation of microstructural parameters in 9–12% Cr-steels", International Journal of Pressure Vessels and Piping 84, pp.62–68, 2007.

102- L. Milovic, T. Vuherer, M. Zrilic, D. Momcilovic, S. Putic, "Microstructural Analysis of Simulated Heat Affected Zone in Creep Resisting Steel", 3rd International Conference on Deformation Processing and Structure of Materials, Belgrade, 2007.

www.ingramcontent.com/pod-product-compliance
Lightning Source LLC
Chambersburg PA
CBHW051146220526
45473CB00003B/674